# Newspapers and Periodicals by and about Black People

*southeastern library holdings*

*A*
*Reference*
*Publication*
*in*
*Black Studies*

Dorothy Porter
*Editor*

## AFRICAN-AMERICAN MATERIALS PROJECT STAFF

Director                                          Annette L. Phinazee
Associate Director, 1971-1973            Geraldine O. Matthews
Assistant Director, 1973-1974             Carol J. Hall
Library Assistant                            Helena M. Wynn

## PARTICIPANTS

Atlanta University                              Casper L. Jordan, *Editor*
Fisk University                                   Jesse C. Smith
Hampton Institute                             Jason C. Grant, III
North Carolina Central University      Pennie E. Perry
South Carolina State College          Lillie S. Walker
Tuskegee Institute                            Annie G. King

# Newspapers and Periodicals by and about Black People

## southeastern library holdings

Compiled by the
### AFRICAN-AMERICAN MATERIALS PROJECT STAFF
School of Library Science, North Carolina Central University
Durham, North Carolina

*Assisted by*
Lillie Dailey Caster

## G.K.HALL&CO.

70 LINCOLN STREET, BOSTON, MASS.

*Library of Congress Cataloging in Publication Data*
North Carolina Central University. School of Library
  Science. African-American Materials Project.
  Newspapers and periodicals by and about Black people.

  (A Reference publication in Black studies)
    1. Afro-Americans — Periodicals — Bibliography — Union
lists.    2. Afro-American periodicals — Bibliography — Union
lists.    3. Afro-American newspapers — Bibliography —
Union lists.    4. Blacks — Periodicals — Bibliography —
Union lists.    5. Catalogs, Union — Southern States.
I. Title.
Z1361.N39N67    1978    [E185.5]    016.30145'196    78-15625
ISBN 0-8161-8264-7

*This publication is printed on permanent/durable acid-free paper*
MANUFACTURED IN THE UNITED STATES OF AMERICA

# Foreword

A preliminary edition of a census of newspapers and
periodicals by and about Black people is presented here.
The emphasis is placed on preliminary as the list repre-
sents an attempt to locate the many ephemeral, often
evanescent, copies of materials long neglected in the
American'cultural and intellectual history. The list is
one product of the unfinished tasks of the African American Materials Project (AAMP).

AAMP was funded by the United States Office of Education, 1971-1974, and through the good offices of the
School of Library Science of the North Carolina Central
University in Durham, a pioneer effort was made to docu-
ment the Black experience in six Southeastern states.
Librarians in predominantly and historically Black academic institutions in the six states (Virginia, North
Carolina, South Carolina, Georgia, Alabama, and Tennessee)
served as state coordinators and were given the opportunity to locate and describe holdings in their respective
states. Emphasis was placed on locating newspapers and
periodicals, pre-1950 monograph imprints, archives and
manuscripts, and academic theses. Unfortunately, the
lack of additional funding precluded the completion of
the Project.

Very little attention has been given to Black serials.
Armistead S. Pride provided a selected list of Black
newspapers for the Library of Congress' microfilm project in 1953. In 1946 Warren H. Brown published a
Checklist of Negro Newspapers in the United States

(1827-1946). The Union List of Serials gives scant
attention to the subject although some libraries do
report their holdings.  None of these attempted to locate copies of these valuable resources in any system-
atic fashion.  Penelope Bullock's Ph.D. dissertation on
Negro periodicals in the United States was a great source
of help.  The indefatigable Dorothy Porter described the
magnificent holdings of serials in the Howard University
library book catalogs.  This would point out the unique-
ness of the present list.

Too much praise cannot be heaped on the staff of
AAMP:  its first associate director Geraldine Matthews
and her successor Carol J. Hall.  These two young women
had the formidable task of drawing together diverse
entries and attempting to bring some uniformity to the
undertaking.  Thanks are also due the state coordinators:

> Alabama - Annie G. King, Librarian, Tuskegee
> Institute
> Georgia - Casper L. Jordan, Associate Professor,
> Atlanta University
> North Carolina - Pennie E. Perry, Librarian,
> North Carolina Central University
> South Carolina - Lillie S. Walker, Acting
> Librarian, South Carolina State
> College
> Tennessee - Jessie C. Smith, University Librarian,
> Fisk University
> Virginia - Jason C. Grant, III, Librarian,
> Hampton Institute.

A special thanks is tendered Annette L. Phinazee, Dean
of the School of Library Science, North Carolina Central
University, for spearheading the Project and finding
time in a busy schedule to offer insights to a much
needed, but misunderstood, project.

Many of the entries could not be verified; this was
especially true for African entries.  Many of the entries
are incomplete as to imprint information and holdings.

*Foreword*

Rather than omit them it was decided to include them to
reveal the titles that have been located; correspondence
with the library can elicit those numbers held.

It is the sincere desire of the participants in AAMP
that the list will be of use to the intellectual
community.

Casper LeRoy Jordan
Associate Professor
Atlanta University School of
     Library Service
                    and
Director, Trevor Arnett Library
Atlanta University Center

# Contents

# Preface

Approximately one thousand titles are included in
Newspapers and Periodicals By and About Black People.
Coverage extends to publications of fraternal orders;
religious denominations; occupational, political, pro-
fessional, and cultural organizations; colleges; students;
and the United States government. Periodicals embrace a
variety of types of serials, including administrative
reports and proceedings. The publications originate in
Africa, the West Indies, Mexico, Haiti, Belgium, France,
India, Spain, the Netherlands, and Great Britain as well
as the United States. Domestic serials are not confined
to those emanating from the Black press.

No additions have been made to the holdings in the
three years since 1974, when AAMP grant funds expired
and the Project staff dispersed. Instead, attention has
been concentrated upon making the format of the entries
conform more consistently to that of the Union List of
Serials, whose format had been adopted initially as a
model. Corrections have been made within the limits of
time and resources available and an attempt has been
made to identify all of the location symbols of the
holding libraries. A separate list has been made of
location symbols for which the names of the corresponding
reporting institutions are lacking. It is possible that
some of these symbols are typographical errors, but this
could not be ascertained. It seemed useful, nevertheless,
to include the symbols in the several entries and to list
them separately with the hope that they could be identi-
fied and corrected later.

*Preface*

Users should be aware of the major limitations of the list. Mr. Jordan has already called attention to these. Regrettably, the list includes errors and unverified entries. However, these limitations may be offset considerably when the following are taken into account.

The compilation is unique in providing both intellectual and physical access to a "cross section" of serial publications in a particular geographical area by and about Black people. One hundred and eighty-three cooperating libraries from the six Southeastern states are represented in the present compilation as compared with 38 which are included in that basic retrospective source, the Union List of Serials, as shown in Table I. One hundred and fifty-three more locations become available.

TABLE I

Comparison of Libraries listed in
Union List of Serials and in
Newspapers and Periodicals By and About Black People

| | Libraries in | | | Libraries not in Union List of Serials |
| | Union List of Serials | Newspapers & Periods. By & ... | Both Lists | |
| States | | | | |
|---|---|---|---|---|
| Alabama | 9 | 4 | 2 | 2 |
| Georgia | 18 | 5 | 2 | 3 |
| North Carolina | 19 | 45 | 7 | 38 |
| South Carolina | 5 | 17 | 3 | 14 |
| Tennessee | 18 | 38 | 6 | 32 |
| Virginia | 15 | 74 | 10 | 64 |
| Total | 38 | 183 | 30 | 153 |

## *Preface*

When the 89 titles beginning with the letter C and
the 110 beginning with N that are in this compilation
were searched, only 26 titles among the C entries and 41
among the N entries were found in the Union List of
Serials. A few of the titles beginning with these letters
were outside the scope of ULS. The entries in C and N
were chosen for testing, because the long history of
Black serials whose titles begin with the words colored,
national, or Negro suggested the likelihood that they
would be held by libraries reporting to ULS, particularly
large research institutions and those which are predominantly Black.

The compilation, then, reveals the rich resources of
the six states and opens new avenues for locating specific works for research and interlibrary loan. Knowing
what materials exist and where they are located are
essential to scholars.

One or two aspects of the union list of Black serials
deserve attention. Among periodicals, Crisis (1910),*
Jet (1950), Journal of Negro History (1916), Negro
Digest/Black World (1943), Negro History Bulletin (1937),
Journal of Negro Education (1932), and Phylon (1940) are
the staples, being those most frequently held by the
reporting libraries of the six states. Black Enterprise
(1970), Black Scholar (1969), Freedomways (1961), and
Journal of African History (1960) are among the runners
up in the periodical field. The long established Afro-
American (1892), Chicago Defender (1905), Journal and
Guide (1899), and Pittsburgh Courier (1910) are the
newspapers most often found in the cooperating libraries.

The evolution of a group name may be observed from
certain titles in the compilation. Specific terms reflect
contemporary thought. Eleven newspapers and periodicals
begin with the word colored. All were founded in the
19th century or the early decades of the 20th century
when colored was widely used as the term of racial

---

*Founding dates are in parentheses.

identification. The first word of 38 titles is Negro, the appellation resulting from a campaign in the twenties and thirties to promote its use as a badge of respect. Negro appeared as first title word as early as the first decade of the 20th century. Usage within titles and as first word reached its height in the fourth and fifth decades and began its decline in the sixth as Black started its rise toward currency as the group name. Those espousing Black based their choice on ideology, rejecting Negro for its connections with slavery and segregation. Once considered a derogatory term, Black seems to be the current preferred racial designation. Forty-one entries beginning with Black attest to its acceptability. Of the 31 dated entries with Black as first title word, founding dates for 10 were in 1965 or the later sixties and for 18 during the seventies. One of the latter, originally beginning with Negro, changed its name to conform to the new ideologically based terminology. The less frequently used racial designations, Afro-American and Soul, appear as initial title words in four and three entries respectively.

The titles of newspapers and periodicals mirror social issues and concerns. The very first Black newspaper, Freedom's Journal, born in 1827, pleaded freedom's cause. The abolitionist movement is seen in titles beginning with or containing the words anti-slavery and abolition. In more recent times, the freedom movement of the nineteen sixties spawned Freedomways. Other titles are expressive: Emancipator, Liberator, Equal Opportunity, Civil Rights Digest, as are other title words such as interracial, advocate, argus, crusader, tribune, and human relations. Works such as the Journal of Negro History bring the findings of historical research to attention, filling a void in the study of American History. Other works such as African Studies Review and Journal of Black Studies support today's curricula in institutions of higher education and broaden the dimensions of the Black experience.

Issuance of Newspapers and Periodicals By and About Black People as a preliminary edition should have a

*Preface*

salutary effect on further cooperation and cooperative
planning. First, in offering a comprehensive view of
holdings, the list facilitates the identification of
gaps and thus gives guidance in filling them in. Second,
the list provides opportunities for librarians as they
use it to assist with the correction and verification of
entries. Cooperation in this respect is earnestly sought
and is essential to bring about a complete edition. Corrections, etc., should be addressed to:

> Dean
> School of Library Science
> North Carolina Central University
> Durham, N. C. 27707

Third, one kind of cooperative effort should be the out-
lining and pursuing of a plan which would provide for
the continual updating of the original list. Fourth, it
is hoped that the publication of this retrospective list
of Black newspapers and periodicals will spur librarians
to come together again in a new and enlarged cooperative
endeavor for identifying, locating, collecting, purchas-
ing, and preserving these forms of materials. These
concerns represent an important agenda for the librarians
of the Southeastern region. Let it not be said that the
enormous cooperative effort exerted in compiling <u>News-
papers and Periodicals By and About Black People</u> ends
with its publication.

The fact is, that despite its major limitations, this
union list is a significant contribution to the literature of the Black experience. In so far as can be
ascertained, nowhere does there exist a comparable record
of serials holdings relating to Black people. The
Director of the African-American Materials Project, the
staff, and the cooperating libraries deserve deep grati-
tude for their yeoman service.

> Lillie D. Caster
> Head Cataloger
> D. H. Hill Library
> North Carolina State University

# Explanation of Entries

Newspapers and periodicals are arranged in one alphabet.

## Bibliographical Data

Each entry includes as much of the following data as was available at the time of compilation:

1. Name of issuing body in parentheses following the title.
2. Place of publication.
3. Beginning and ending volumes and dates.
   If still being published, a plus sign follows the date.
   If ceased publication, the parallel follows the date.
   If date of cessation is uncertain, a question mark follows the parallel.
4. Frequency of publication (See Abbreviations).
5. Notes describing relationships.

## Holdings

Holdings are shown in summarized form by volume numbering or dates following the location symbol of each library. A location symbol alone may mean (1) holdings are of current issues, or retained for short periods

only; (2) holdings consist of scattered issues; or
(3) holdings were not listed by the reporting library.
Virginia is an exception to no. 3.   A symbol alone for a
Virginia library indicates a complete file.

+   A plus sign at the end of holdings means cur-
    rently received from the last volume or date.
()  Parentheses indicate that the enclosed vol-
    umes or years are incomplete.
MF  The letters MF indicate holdings are in
    microform.

# Abbreviations

| | | | |
|---|---|---|---|
| Ag | August | My | May |
| Ap | April | N | November |
| d | daily | no | number |
| D | December | ns | new series |
| F | February | O | October |
| Ja | January | s | series |
| Je | June | S | September |
| Jl | July | tw | twice weekly |
| MF | Microform | v | volume |
| Mr | March | w | weekly |

# Key to Location Symbols

| Location Symbol | Institution and Address |
|---|---|
| A-AR | ALABAMA. DEPARTMENT OF ARCHIVES AND HISTORY<br>Montgomery, Alabama  36104 |
| ATT | TUSKEGEE INSTITUTE<br>Tuskegee Institute, Alabama  36088 |
| AU | UNIVERSITY OF ALABAMA<br>University, Alabama  35486 |
| GA | ATLANTA PUBLIC LIBRARY<br>Atlanta, Georgia  30303 |
| GACC | CLARK COLLEGE<br>Atlanta, Georgia  30314 |
| GAMB | MORRIS BROWN COLLEGE<br>Atlanta, Georgia 30314 |
| GASC | SPELMAN COLLEGE<br>Atlanta, Georgia  30314 |
| GAU | ATLANTA UNIVERSITY<br>Atlanta, Georgia  30314 |

# Key to Location Symbols

NcALB      STANLEY COUNTY PUBLIC LIBRARY
Albemarle, North Carolina 28001

NcAsbC      RANDOLPH COUNTY LIBRARY
Asheboro, North Carolina 27203

NcBE      BELMONT-ABBEY COLLEGE
Belmont, North Carolina 28012

NcBoA      APPALACHIAN STATE UNIVERSITY
Boone, North Carolina 28607

NcBuC      CAMPBELL COLLEGE
Buies Creek, North Carolina 27506

NcCJ      JOHNSON C. SMITH UNIVERSITY
Charlotte, North Carolina 28216

NcCO      CONCORD PUBLIC LIBRARY
Concord, North Carolina 28025

NcCoB      BARBER-SCOTIA COLLEGE
Concord, North Carolina 28025

NcCQ      QUEENS COLLEGE
Charlotte, North Carolina 28207

NcCU      UNIVERSITY OF NORTH CAROLINA
AT CHARLOTTE
Charlotte, North Carolina 28223

NcCuW      WESTERN CAROLINA UNIVERSITY
Cullowhee, North Carolina 28723

NcD      DUKE UNIVERSITY
Durham, North Carolina 27706

NcDaD      DAVIDSON COLLEGE
Davidson, North Carolina 28036

NcDur      DURHAM CITY-COUNTY PUBLIC LIBRARY
Durham, North Carolina 27702

## Key to Location Symbols

NcDurC            NORTH CAROLINA CENTRAL UNIVERSITY
Durham, North Carolina 27707

NcEC              EDGECOMBE COUNTY MEMORIAL LIBRARY
Tarboro, North Carolina 27886

NcElcU            ELIZABETH CITY STATE UNIVERSITY
Elizabeth City, North Carolina 27909

NcFayC            CUMBERLAND COUNTY PUBLIC LIBRARY
Fayetteville, North Carolina 28302

NcFayS            FAYETTEVILLE STATE UNIVERSITY
Fayetteville, North Carolina 28301

NcFB              U.S. FORT BRAGG MAIN POST LIBRARY
Fort Bragg, North Carolina 28307

NcGO             WAYNE COUNTY PUBLIC LIBRARY
Goldsboro, North Carolina 27530

NcGrE             EAST CAROLINA UNIVERSITY
Greenville, North Carolina 27834

NcGrS             SHEPPARD MEMORIAL LIBRARY
Greenville, North Carolina 27834

NcGU             UNIVERSITY OF NORTH CAROLINA AT
GREENSBORO
Greensboro, North Carolina 27412

NcGuG            GUILFORD COLLEGE
Greensboro, North Carolina 27410

NcHP              HIGH POINT PUBLIC LIBRARY
High Point, North Carolina 27261

NcHY              ELBERT IVEY MEMORIAL LIBRARY
Hickory, North Carolina 28601

NcHyL             LENOIR RHYNE COLLEGE
Hickory, North Carolina 28601

# Key to Location Symbols

NcL          SCOTLAND COUNTY MEMORIAL LIBRARY
Laurinburg, North Carolina  28352

NcLK         ROCKINGHAM COUNTY LIBRARY
Eden, North Carolina  27288

NcMip        PFEIFFER COLLEGE
Misenheimer, North Carolina  28109

NcMV         MOORESVILLE PUBLIC LIBRARY
Mooresville, North Carolina  28115

NcPC         PASQUOTANK-CAMDEN LIBRARY
Elizabeth City, North Carolina  27909

NcRM         THOMAS HACKNEY BRASWELL MEMORIAL
LIBRARY
Rocky Mount, North Carolina  27801

NcRo         ROCKINGHAM-RICHMOND COUNTY LIBRARY
Rockingham, North Carolina  28379

NcRR         RICHARD B. HARRISON PUBLIC LIBRARY
Raleigh, North Carolina  27610

NcRS         NORTH CAROLINA STATE UNIVERSITY
Raleigh, North Carolina  27607

NcRSA        ST. AUGUSTINE'S COLLEGE
Raleigh, North Carolina  27611

NcRSH        SHAW UNIVERSITY
Raleigh, North Carolina  27610

NcSalC       CATAWBA COLLEGE
Salisbury, North Carolina  28144

NcSalL       LIVINGSTONE COLLEGE
Salisbury, North Carolina  28144

NcU          UNIVERSITY OF NORTH CAROLINA
Chapel Hill, North Carolina  27514

## Key to Location Symbols

NcWS          FORSYTH COUNTY PUBLIC LIBRARY
Winston-Salem, North Carolina  27101

NcWU          UNIVERSITY OF NORTH CAROLINA AT
WILMINGTON
Wilmington, North Carolina  28401

NcY            HYCONEECHEE REGIONAL LIBRARY, INC.
Yanceyville, North Carolina  27379

ScCLEA        CLEMSON UNIVERSITY
Clemson, South Carolina  29631

ScCLP          PRESBYTERIAN COLLEGE
Clinton, South Carolina  29325

ScCOB          BENEDICT COLLEGE
Columbia, South Carolina  29204

ScCOC          COLUMBIA COLLEGE
Columbia, South Carolina  29203

ScCSM          OLD SLAVE MART MUSEUM AND CRAFTS
Charleston, South Carolina  29401

S.D. Bishop    S.D. BISHOP STATE JUNIOR COLLEGE
Mobile, Alabama  36603

ScDWE          ERSKINE COLLEGE
Due West, South Carolina  29639

ScGAL          LIMESTONE COLLEGE
Gaffney, South Carolina  29340

ScGRVF        FURMAN UNIVERSITY
Greenville, South Carolina  29613

ScHaC          COKER COLLEGE
Hartsville, South Carolina  29550

ScNC           NEWBERRY COLLEGE
Newberry, South Carolina  29108

## Key to Location Symbols

ScOrC      CLAFLIN COLLEGE
Orangeburg, South Carolina   29115

ScOrS      SOUTH CAROLINA STATE COLLEGE
Orangeburg, South Carolina   29115

ScRHW      WINTHROP COLLEGE
Rock Hill, South Carolina   29730

ScSPC      CONVERSE COLLEGE
Spartanburg, South Carolina   29301

ScSpW      WOFFORD COLLEGE
Spartanburg, South Carolina   29301

ScU      UNIVERSITY OF SOUTH CAROLINA
Columbia, South Carolina   29208

TD      DICKSON COUNTY PUBLIC LIBRARY
Dickson, Tennessee   37055

TG      GREENE COUNTY LIBRARY
Greeneville, Tennessee   37743

TJeCN      CARSON-NEWMAN COLLEGE
Jefferson City, Tennessee   37760

TJoS      EAST TENNESSEE STATE UNIVERSITY
Johnson City, Tennessee   37601

TKL      KNOXVILLE PUBLIC LIBRARY SYSTEM
Knoxville, Tennessee   37902

TLC      CUMBERLAND COLLEGE OF TENNESSEE
Lebanon, Tennessee   37087

TMaU      UNIVERSITY OF TENNESSEE AT MARTIN
Martin, Tennessee   38237

TMeVH      U.S. VETERANS ADMINISTRATION HOSPITAL
Memphis, Tennessee   38104

## Key to Location Symbols

TMMH
METHODIST HOSPITAL SCHOOL OF NURSING
Memphis, Tennessee 38104

TMMU
UNIVERSITY OF TENNESSEE MEDICAL UNITS
LIBRARY
Memphis, Tennessee 38163

TMNH
MEMPHIS NAVAL HOSPITAL
Memphis, Tennessee 38054

TMS
MEMPHIS PUBLIC LIBRARY - SOUTH BRANCH
Memphis, Tennessee 38104

TM-SW
SOUTHWESTERN AT MEMPHIS
Memphis, Tennessee 38112

TMU
MIDDLE TENNESSEE STATE UNIVERSITY
Murfreesboro, Tennessee 37130

TN
NASHVILLE PUBLIC LIBRARY
Nashville, Tennessee 37203

TNB
MID-SOUTH BIBLE COLLEGE
Memphis, Tennessee 38112

TNBK
KING COLLEGE
Bristol, Tennessee 37620

TNBSB
BAPTIST SUNDAY SCHOOL BOARD
Nashville, Tennessee 37203

TND
DAVID LIPSCOMB COLLEGE
Nashville, Tennessee 37203

TNDC
DISCIPLES OF CHRIST HISTORICAL SOCIETY
LIBRARY
Nashville, Tennessee 37212

TN-E
NASHVILLE PUBLIC LIBRARY - EDGEHILL
BRANCH
Nashville, Tennessee 37203

## Key to Location Symbols

TNF
FISK UNIVERSITY
Nashville, Tennessee   37203

TN-H
NASHVILLE PUBLIC LIBRARY - HADLEY
PARK BRANCH
Nashville, Tennessee   37208

TNJ
JOINT UNIVERSITIES LIBRARIES
Nashville, Tennessee   37203

TNJ-S
SCARRITT COLLEGE
Nashville, Tennessee   37203

TNK
KNOXVILLE COLLEGE
Knoxville, Tennessee   37921

TNL
LANE COLLEGE
Jackson, Tennessee   38301

TNLO
LEMOYNE-OWEN COLLEGE
Memphis, Tennessee   38126

TNMa
MARYVILLE COLLEGE
Maryville, Tennessee   37801

TNMe
MEMPHIS STATE UNIVERSITY
Memphis, Tennessee   38152

TNMH
MORRISTOWN-HAMBLEN LIBRARY
Morristown, Tennessee   37814

TNT
TREVECCA NAZARENE COLLEGE
Nashville, Tennessee   37211

TNW
TENNESSEE WESLEYAN COLLEGE
Athens, Tennessee   37303

TOR
OAKRIDGE PUBLIC LIBRARY
Oakridge, Tennessee   37830

TPM
MARTIN COLLEGE
Palaski, Tennessee

## Key to Location Symbols

TRR            RACE RELATIONS INFORMATION CENTER
Nashville, Tennessee  37212

TTM            MOTLOW STATE COMMUNITY COLLEGE
Tullahoma, Tennessee  37388

TWOH          ORENA HUMPHREY PUBLIC LIBRARY
Whitwell, Tennessee  37397

VBpL          BEDFORD PUBLIC LIBRARY
Bedford, Virginia  24523

VBrC          BRIDGEWATER COLLEGE
Alexander Mark Memorial Library
Bridgewater, Virginia  22812

VBrP          BRISTOL PUBLIC LIBRARY
Bristol, Virginia  24201

VBgR         BRUNSWICK GREENVILLE REGIONAL LIBRARY
Lawrenceville, Virginia  23868

VChT         CHARLES H. TAYLOR MEMORIAL LIBRARY
4205 Victoria Boulevard
Hampton, Virginia  23369

VClV         CLINCH VALLEY COLLEGE OF THE UNIVERSITY
OF VIRGINIA
John Cook Wythe Library
Wise, Virginia  24293

VCnC         CHRISTOPHER NEWPORT COLLEGE OF THE
COLLEGE OF WILLIAM AND MARY
Newport News, Virginia  23606

VCoU         VIRGINIA COMMONWEALTH UNIVERSITY
James Branch Cabell Library
Richmond, Virginia  23220

VCpL         CHESAPEAKE PUBLIC LIBRARY
Chesapeake, Virginia  23320

## Key to Location Symbols

VCrR        CENTRAL RAPPAHANNOCK REGIONAL LIBRARY
Fredericksburg, Virginia  22401

VCvC        CENTRAL VIRGINIA COMMUNITY COLLEGE
Wards Road South, P. O. Box 4098
Fort Hill Station, Lynchburg,
Virginia  24502

VCwM        COLLEGE OF WILLIAM AND MARY
Earl Gregg Swem Library
Williamsburg, Virginia  23185

VDcC        DANVILLE COMMUNITY COLLEGE
Danville, Virginia  24541

VDpL        DEPARTMENT OF PUBLIC LIBRARIES
City of Virginia Beach
Virginia Beach, Virginia  33456

VFcL        FALLS CHURCH PUBLIC LIBRARY
Falls Church, Virginia  22046

VFeC        FERRUM COLLEGE
Ferrum, Virginia  24088

VFgM        FAIRFAX COUNTY PUBLIC LIBRARY
George Mason Regional Library
Annandale, Virginia  22003

VFpH        FAIRFAX COUNTY PUBLIC LIBRARY
Patrick Henry Branch
Vienna, Virginia  22180

VFpR        FRANKLIN-PATRICK REGIONAL LIBRARY
Stuart, Virginia  24171

VFrB        FAIRFAX COUNTY PUBLIC LIBRARY
Richard Byrd Branch
Springfield, Virginia  22150

VFsP        FORT STORY POST LIBRARY
Virginia Beach, Virginia  23459

## Key to Location Symbols

VFsR        FAIRFAX COUNTY PUBLIC LIBRARY
Sherwood Regional Library
Alexandria, Virginia  22306

VFwW        FAIRFAX COUNTY PUBLIC LIBRARY
Woodrow Wilson Branch
Falls Church, Virginia  22046

VGmC        GEORGE MASON COLLEGE OF THE UNIVERSITY
OF VIRGINIA
Fenwick Library
Fairfax, Virginia  22030

VHaI        HAMPTON INSTITUTE
Collis P. Huntington Memorial Library
Hampton, Virginia  23368

VHcC        VIRGINIA HIGHLANDS COMMUNITY COLLEGE
P. O. Box 828
Abingdon, Virginia  24210

VHcS        HALIFAX COUNTY-SOUTH BOSTON REGIONAL
LIBRARY
Halifax, Virginia  24558

VHfB        HENRICO COUNTY PUBLIC LIBRARY
Fairfield Branch
Richmond, Virginia  23227

VHoC        HOLLIS COLLEGE
Fishburn Library
Hollis College, Virginia  24020

VHsC        HAMPDEN-SYDNEY COLLEGE
Hampden-Sydney, Virginia  23943

VKpL        KIRN PUBLIC LIBRARY
Norfolk, Virginia  23510

VLaF        LANGLEY AFB LIBRARY
Hampton, Virginia  23365

## Key to Location Symbols

VLpL            LYNCHBURG PUBLIC LIBRARY
Lynchburg, Virginia   24504

VMaC           MADISON COLLEGE LIBRARY
Madison College
Harrisonburg, Virginia   22801

VMcV           MARYMOUNT COLLEGE OF VIRGINIA
Ireton Library
Arlington, Virginia   22207

VMoC           MARY BALDWIN COLLEGE
Staunton, Virginia   24401

VMmL           MORGAN MEMORIAL LIBRARY
Suffolk, Virginia   23434

VMpL           MCINTIRE PUBLIC LIBRARY (BRANCH)
Charlottesville, Virginia   22903

VMuC           VIRGINIA MUSEUM OF THE CONFEDERACY
1201 East Clay Street
Richmond, Virginia   23219

VMwC           MARY WASHINGTON COLLEGE
E. Lee Trinkle Library
Fredericksburg, Virginia   22401

VNaB           NAVAL AMPHIBIOUS BASE LIBRARY
Norfolk, Virginia   23521

VNnP           NEWPORT NEWS PUBLIC LIBRARY SYSTEM
Newport News, Virginia   23601

VNnS           NEWPORT NEWS SHIPBUILDING AND DRY DOCK
COMPANY
Technical Information Center
Newport News, Virginia   23607

VNsC           NORFOLK STATE COLLEGE
Norfolk, Virginia   23504

## Key to Location Symbols

VOcP       ORANGE COUNTY PUBLIC LIBRARY
Orange, Virginia  22960

Vorhees       VORHEES COLLEGE
Denmark, South Carolina  29042

VPcL       PULASKI COUNTY LIBRARY
Pulaski, Virginia  24301

VPhC       PATRICK HENRY COMMUNITY COLLEGE
Martinsville, Virginia  24112

VPpL       PORTSMOUTH PUBLIC LIBRARY
Portsmouth, Virginia  23704

VPuL       PURCELLVILLE LIBRARY
Purcellville, Virginia  22132

VPwC       PRINCE WILLIAM COUNTY PUBLIC LIBRARY
Manassas, Virginia  22110

VRaC       RADFORD COLLEGE
John Preston McConnell Library
Radford, Virginia  24141

VRbC       RICHARD BLAND COLLEGE OF THE COLLEGE
OF WILLIAM AND MARY
Petersburg, Virginia  23803

VRcP       ROANOKE COUNTY PUBLIC LIBRARY
Salem, Virginia  24153

VRmC       RANDOLPH-MACON COLLEGE
Walter Hines Page Library
Ashland, Virginia  23005

VRmW       RANDOLPH-MACON WOMAN'S COLLEGE
Lynchburg, Virginia  24502

VRoP       ROANOKE PUBLIC LIBRARY
Gainsboro Branch
Roanoke, Virginia  24016

## Key to Location Symbols

VRpL         RICHMOND PUBLIC LIBRARY
Richmond, Virginia  23219

VSbC         SWEET BRIAR COLLEGE
Mary Helen Cochran Library
Sweet Briar, Virginia  24595

VSpL         STAUNTON PUBLIC LIBRARY
Staunton, Virginia  24401

VSrL         SOUTHSIDE REGIONAL LIBRARY
Boydton, Virginia  23917

VSsH         SOUTHWESTERN STATE HOSPITAL LIBRARY
Marion, Virginia  24354

VStC         VIRGINIA STATE COLLEGE
Ettrick, Virginia  23803

VStL         VIRGINIA STATE LIBRARY
12th and Capitol Streets
Richmond, Virginia  23219

VSuC         SULLINS COLLEGE
Bristol, Virginia  24201

VTnC         THOMAS NELSON COMMUNITY COLLEGE
Drawer "K", Riverdale Station
Hampton, Virginia  23336

VUnR         UNIVERSITY OF RICHMOND
Richmond, Virginia  23220

VUnU         VIRGINIA UNION UNIVERSITY
1500 N. Lombardy Street
Richmond, Virginia  23220

VUnV         UNIVERSITY OF VIRGINIA
Alderman Library
Charlottesville, Virginia  22901

## Key to Location Symbols

VUsN                    U.S. NAVAL AIR STATION LIBRARY
                        Norfolk, Virginia   28511

VUtS                    UNION THEOLOGICAL SEMINARY
                        Richmond, Virginia   23227

VUvS                    UNIVERSITY OF VIRGINIA
                        Medical Library
                        School of Medicine
                        Charlottesville, Virginia   22901

VVaC                    VETERANS ADMINISTRATION CENTER LIBRARY
                        Hampton, Virginia   23367

VWcC                    WYTHEVILLE COMMUNITY COLLEGE LIBRARY
                        Wytheville, Virginia   24382

VWpL                    WAYNESBORO PUBLIC LIBRARY
                        Waynesboro, Virginia   22980

LOCATION SYMBOLS for which the names of participating
libraries could not be located

| | |
|---|---|
| AAM | TK |
| APL | TKM |
| NcBoC | TMH |
| NcET | TMVH |
| NcLA | TNBPB |
| ScGORC | TNMO |
| TD | TNSPB |
| TDB | TNVH |
| TJL | TS-M |

# Newspapers and Periodicals by and about Black People

AACC BULLETIN.
    (All Africa Conference of Churches) Kitwe, Zambia.
    v1-4, no3, O 1963-Je 1967//
       TNJ-S 1-4

ABA JOURNAL.
       TNF

A. M. E. CHURCH REVIEW.
    (African Methodist Episcopal Church) Philadelphia.
    1, Jl 1884+
       GAMB 80, 92
       TNF (3), 6-7, (20), (39), 62, (63), (69)
       VHaI 16-20, 23, 25, 28-31

AMSAC NEWSLETTER.
    (American Society of African Culture) New York.
    v1-8, no1, 1958-F 1966
       GAU 1-7
       NcRR (1-6)
       TNF 8
       VHaI (2), (4)-5, (7)

ABBOTT'S MONTHLY.
    Chicago. v1-7, no3, O 1930-S 1933//
       GAU (1)
       TNF (1), (2), 3

ABOLITION INTELLIGENCER AND MISSIONARY MAGAZINE.
Shelbyville, Kentucky.  v1, no1-12, My 1822-Ap 1823//
ScU MF

ABOLITIONIST.
Boston.  v1, no1-12, Ja-D 1833//
ScU MF

ACT.
Chicago.  1, O 1946+
TNF 44, 46

ACTIVITY STUDY BOOK FOR INTERMEDIATES.
Nashville.
TNSPB

ACTIVITY STUDY BOOK FOR JUNIORS.
Nashville.
TNSPB

ADULT BIBLE QUARTERLY.
Nashville.
TNSPB

ADVANCED BIBLE STUDIES.
Nashville.
TNSPB

ADVOCATE OF PEACE AND THE CHRISTIAN PATRIOT.
Philadelphia.  v1, no1-12, S 1828-Je 1829//
ScU MF

ADVOCATE OF PEACE AND UNIVERSAL BROTHERHOOD.
Boston.  v1-6, ns v1-12, 1837-1850
ScU MF

ADVOCATE OF THE PEOPLE'S RIGHTS.
(Early state records series) Brazoria, Texas.  v1,
no8, F 1934//
ScU MF

AFRAMERICAN WOMAN'S JOURNAL.
   (National Council of Negro Women) Washington, D. C.
   vl-8, 1940-1949//?
      TNF

AFRICA (Current History).
      VNsC 1972+

AFRICA.
   (International Institute of African Languages and
   Cultures) London.  vl-13, no3, Ja 1928-Jl 1940//
   v14, 1943+
      AAM 38
      ATT 1+
      NcBoA 41
      NcBuC
      NcCoB
      NcRR 32-44
      ScGRVF 38+
      ScOrS 41+
      ScRHW 38+
      ScU 1-41
      TM-SW 25
      TNF 1-4, 6
         10-13, 14
         15-40, 16
      TNJ-S 1+
      TNMe 1+
      VcwM 33+
      VHaI 8+
      VNsC 1-36 1972+
      VRmW 38+
      VUnV
      VUtS 32+

AFRICA CONFIDENTIAL.
   London.  vl, 1960+  See also African Confidential
      NcDurC 1+
      ScRHW 8-9
      TNJ-S 1+
      VCwM 11+

AFRICA DIARY.
    New Delhi, India.  vl, 1961+
        VCwM 1+
        VNsC 6+

AFRICA DIGEST.
    (Africa Bureau) London.  vl-21, Jl 1952-1974//
        NcBoA 18+
        NcDurC 5+
        NcElcU 16
        NcRR 10-16
        TNF 2-4, 7-19
        VHaI (10-12)-(15-17)+
        VNsC 17+

AFRICA FIELD NEWS.
        TNDC

AFRICA FORUM.
        AAM

AFRICA INSTITUTE BULLETIN.
    Pretoria, South Africa.  vl, 1963+
        NcDurC 1
        ScRHW 2+
        TNJ-S (1)+
        VUnV (1-7), 8

AFRICA NOW.
    New York.
        TNJ-S

AFRICA PULSE.
        TNJ-S (1)-

AFRICA REPORT.
    (African-American Institute) Washington, D. C.  1,
    Jl 5, 1956+
        ATT 7+
        GA
        NcCoB
        NcDad

(AFRICA REPORT.)
      NcDur
      NcElcU 9-13
      NcFayS
      NcRR
      NcRSH
      ScCLEA 12+
      ScCLP 1+
      ScCOB 14
      ScDWE (1), 3
      ScGRVF 13+
      ScNC
      ScOrC 10-11
      ScOrS 7-9
      ScRHW 7-8
      TM-SW 13
      TMU
      TNF (6), 7-9, (10), (11), 12-17
      TNJ-S 2-11, (12-14), 15+
      TNMe 10
      VCnC 17+
      VHaI (1), (3), (5), (12-14)+
      VHcC (14-15)
      VHoC (15)+
      VMaC (9)+
      VNsC 9+
      VRmW 7+
      VRPL 13-(14)+
      VRsR 16+
      VUtS (1-3)+

AFRICA RESEARCH BULLETIN.
    Devon, England. v1, 1964+
      ATT 5
      NcGU
      TNJ-S 1-5, (6), 7

AFRICA RESEARCH LIMITED.
    Exeter, England. 1964?-1968
      TNJ-S

AFRICA SOUTH IN EXILE.
    Capetown, South Africa.  v1-6, no1, O/D 1956-
    J1/S 1960//  (Formerly:  Africa South)
        ATT 1+
        NcDurC 1-6
        TNF
        VHaI (1-2)-5
        VNsC 3-5
        VUnV (1)

AFRICA TODAY.
    (International Race Relations Center) Denver,
    Colorado.  v17, 1970+
        NcCoB 12-14
        NcDurC 9+
        NcRR 9+
        ScCLEA 12+
        ScCLP (15)+
        ScCOB (8-10)+
        ScCOC 15+
        ScGRVF (15)+
        ScNC 15+
        ScOrC (11)+
        ScOrS 14-17 MF
        TNF (4), 5-6, (7), (8-9), (10), 11, 12
        TNJ-S 7+
        TNMe 1
        VHaI 18+
        VMbC 17+
        VNsC 1-11, (15-16)-18+
        VUnV 1-11, (12-16), 17

AFRICA TODAY AND TOMORROW.
        TNF

AFRICA TRADE AND DEVELOPMENT.
    See also:  New Africa
        TNF

AFRICAN.
    (African Christian Mission)
        TNDC

AFRICAN; JOURNAL OF AFRICAN AFFAIRS.
    (Universal Ethiopian Students Association) New York.
    v1-2, no1, O 1937-O 1938//
        TNF (1-2), (7-8)
        VHaI (1-5)

AFRICAN ABSTRACTS.
    (International African Institute).
        ATT 1+
        NcBoA 2-16, 21
        NcRR 14-18
        ScU 1-20
        TNF 1+
        TNJ-S 1+
        TNMe
        VHaI
        VNsC 20+
        VUnV 1-21

AFRICAN ACCENT.
        TNDC

AFRICAN ADULT EDUCATION.
    (Adult Education Association of East and Central
    Africa) Oxford, England. Je 1967+
        TNJ-S 1

AFRICAN AFFAIRS.
    (Royal African Society) London. v1, O 1901+, v1-43,
    no1-71, O 1901-Ap 1944 as the Society's Journal
    (O 1901-Ap 1935 under the society's earlier name:
    African Society)
        ATT 6-23, 57+
        GAU 51
        NcBoA 69
        NcDurC 67
        ScCLEA 65+
        ScOrS 70
        ScRHW 43-64
        ScU 1-69
        TJeCN 66+
        TNF 44-70

(AFRICAN AFFAIRS.)
> TNJ-S 1-35, (36), 37, (38), 39, (40-41), 42-43,
> (44), 45, (46), 47-64, 67, 69+
> TNMe 43+
> VCwM 1+
> VHaI (48)
> VMaC 68+ MF 1-62
> VNsC 65+
> VUnV 1-69

AFRICAN AND ASIAN STUDIES.
> VNsC

AFRICAN ARTS/ARTS D'AFRIQUE.
> (African Studies Center, UCLA) Los Angeles.  vl,
> 1967+
> > ATT 1+
> > NcCoB
> > NcElcU 3
> > NcFayS
> > NcRSA
> > NcRSH
> > NcSalL
> > ScCOB (2)+
> > TNF (4), (5)
> > TNJ-S 1+
> > TNMe 1
> > TNK
> > VHaI 4+
> > VNsC 2+
> > VRaC 2+

AFRICAN BREEZE.
> (Namwianga Mission) Kalomo, Northern Rhodesia.
> > TNDC

AFRICAN CALL.
> TNDC

AFRICAN CHALLENGE.
> Lagos, Nigeria.  1, 1951+

(AFRICAN CHALLENGE.)
    TNJ-S
    VHaI (11-14), (16-17)

AFRICAN CHRISTIAN ADVOCATE.
   (Methodist Church in Africa) Cleveland, Ohio,
   Transvaal? v1, Ap/S 1943+
    TNJ-S 10-12, 13, 27

AFRICAN CONFIDENTIAL.
   London. 1967. (Formerly: Africa Confidential)
    NcDurC 1+

AFRICAN DEVELOPMENT.
   London. 1966+
    VNsC 4+
    VUnV

AFRICAN FORUM.
   (American Society of African Culture) New York.
   v1-3, no4/v4 no1, Summer 1965-Spring/Summer 1968
    ATT 2-4
    NcCoB 1, 4
    NcDurC 1+
    TNF (1-2), 1-5, (6)
    VCwM 1-4
    VHaI 1-2
    VMaC (1)-(4)
    VNsC 1-3

AFRICAN HISTORICAL STUDIES.
   (African Studies Center of Boston University)
   Brookline, Massachusetts. 1, 1968+
    NcSalL 1
    ScCLEA 1+
    TJeCN 3+
    TNJ-S 1
    VCwM 1+

AFRICAN IMAGE.
   (Center for Advanced African Understanding, Inc.)
   Minneapolis, Minnesota. 1 Ja 1969+
    ScCLEA

AFRICAN INSTITUTE BULLETIN.
    NcDurC 1+

AFRICAN INTELLIGENCER.
    (American Colonization Society) Washington, D. C.
    v1, no1, Jl 1820//
        ScU MF

AFRICAN LIBRARY JOURNAL.
        NcElcU 1
        ScCOB
        ScRHW

AFRICAN LITERATURE TODAY.
    London.  v1, 1968+
        VNsC 1+
        VUnV 1+

AFRICAN MESSENGER.
    (Churches of Christ) Louisville, Kentucky.
        TNDC

AFRICAN METHODIST EPISCOPAL CHURCH MAGAZINE.
    Brooklyn, New York.  v1, no1-5, S 1841-D 1842//
        TNF

AFRICAN METHODIST EPISCOPAL ZION QUARTERLY REVIEW.
    Pittsburgh, Pennsylvania.  1, 1888+
        NcSalL 59+

AFRICAN MUSIC.
    (African Music Society) Johannesburg, South Africa.
    1, 1954+
        TM-SW (3)
        TNF

AFRICAN NEWS.
    (Ruth Sloan Associates, Inc.) Washington, D. C.  v1,
    1954
        ATT 2-3
        TNF 1
        VHaI (1-3)

AFRICAN NEWSLETTER.
    (United Christian Missionary Society) Indianapolis.
      TNDC

AFRICAN OBSERVER.
    Philadelphia.  v1, no1-12, Ap 1827-Mr 1828//
      GA 1 MF
      NcDurC
      VHaI 1
      VNsC 1
      VUnV 1-12

AFRICAN OPINION; JOURNAL OF INDEPENDENT THOUGHTS AND
EXPRESSION.
    (African Picture and Information Services) New York.
    v1-5, no11/12, 1 My 1949-Je/Jl 1961; no1/2, 1964+
      NcSalL
      ScCOB (8)+
      TNF 4, (5-10)
      VHaI (1-3)

AFRICAN POLITICAL ORGANIZATION.
    (A. P. O.).  v5, (1913)  See also African Review
      ATT 5

AFRICAN PROGRESS.
    (London).  1, 1960+
      GA
      NcCoB
      NcElcU

AFRICAN QUARTERLY.
    London.  1, 1963+
      TNF (3-6)

AFRICAN RECORDER; A DIGEST OF AFRICAN EVENTS.
    New Delhi, India.  1962+
      VNsC 7+

AFRICAN REPORTS.
      NcRSA

AFRICAN REPOSITORY.
    (American Colonization Society) Washington, D. C.
    v1-68, no1, Mr 1825-Ja 1892// (1-25 as African
    Repository and Colonial Journal. Superseded by
    Liberia: 1-10 in 10)
        GAU 1, 12-14, 16-18, 39, 41, 48-49, 51-52, 67-68
        ScU 1-68 MF
        TNF
        VCwM 1-68
        VHaI (1-8), 12, 14, 16, 19-(21)-(23)-(31-66)
        VMaC 1-68 MF
        VUnV 1-68
        VUtS 1-(13-43)

AFRICAN REVIEW.
    Nairobi, Kenya. v1, 1971+ (Formerly: African
    Political Review. 1969//)
        TNF
        VFsR 1+
        VUnV 1+

AFRICAN SCHOLAR.
    (African Academy of Political and Social Sciences)
    Washington, D. C. 1, Ag/N 1968+
        AAM 1-3
        ATT 1+
        NcCoB (1-2)
        NcSalL 1

AFRICAN SOCIAL RESEARCH.
    Manchester, England. 1944. (Supersedes: Rhodes-
    Livingstone Journal)
        ScRHW 5+
        TJoS
        TNMe

AFRICAN STUDENT'S NEWSLETTER.
    (All African Student's Union of the Americas)
    v1, 1954
        VHaI (1), (4)

AFRICAN STUDIES; A QUARTERLY JOURNAL DEVOTED TO THE
STUDY OF AFRICAN ANTHROPOLOGY, GOVERNMENT AND LANGUAGES.
   Johannesburg, South Africa.  1, Mr 1942+  (Super-
   sedes:  Bantu Studies)
      TNJ-S 1+
      VCwM 1+

AFRICAN STUDIES BULLETIN.
   (African Studies Association) New York.  1 Ap 1958+
      ATT 9+
      GAU 1-6
      NcDurC 1+
      TNF 1-6, 8-14
      TNJ-S (1-7, 10)
      TNMe 1+
      VHaI (5), (12)
      VNsC 12+

AFRICAN STUDIES NEWSLETTER.
   (Brandeis University) Waltham, Massachusetts.  v1,
   1968+
      ScRHW 1+
      TNF
      VHaI 3+

AFRICAN STUDIES REVIEW.
   East Lansing, Michigan.  1958+  (Incorporating:
   African Studies Newsletter)
      ScRHW 10+
      TNF (13), (14)
      VNsC 12+

AFRICAN TIMES AND ORIENT REVIEW.
   London.  1-2, 1912-13, ns v1, no1-22, Mr-Ag 1914//
      ATT 6

AFRICAN WEEKLY.
   New York.  v1, 1957+
      NcDurC 3
      TNF (1-5)

AFRICAN WOMEN.
    (University of London) London.  v1-5, 1954-Je 1963//
       VHaI 1

AFRICAN WORLD.
    London.  1, N, 5 1902+  (Formerly:  African World
    and Cape Cairo Express)
       ATT 22
       NcBuC 22
       NcCoB 21-26
       NcElcU
       S.D. Bishop
       TNF 1-6, (42-45)

AFRICANA.
    Nairobi, Kenya.
       TNF 5, (6), (7)

AFRICANA LIBRARY JOURNAL; A QUARTERLY BIBLIOGRAPHY AND
NEWS BULLETIN.
    New York.  v1, 1970+
       ScOrS 1, (2)
       VHaI 1+
       VUnV 1+

AFRICANA NEWSLETTER.
    Stanford, California.  v1-2, no2, 1962-1964//
    (Absorbed by African Studies Bulletin)
       TNF 1, (2)

AFRICAN'S FRIEND.
    (African's Friend for the Promotion of Religion and
    Morality) Philadelphia.  no1-149, 1886-98//
       ATT
       TNF 1

AFRICA'S LUMINARY.
    (Methodist Episcopal Church) Monrovia, Liberia.
    v1-3, no17, Mr 15 1839-N 19 1841//
       TNJ-S 1

AFRIKA UND UBERSEE.
    Berlin.  1, 0 7, 1910+
        ScU

AFRIQUE NOUVELLE.
    Dakar, Senegal.
        NcDurC (13), (16)

AFRISCOPE.
    Yaba, Nigeria.  1, Je 1971+
        GA

AFROAMERICA.
    (International Institute of Afroamerican Studies)
    Mexico.  v1-2, no3, Ja/Jl 1945-Ja 1946//
        GAU 1

AFROAMERICAN.
    Key Colony Beach, Florida.  1968+
        VCpL 3+
        VNsC 3+

AFRO-AMERICAN.
    (Afro-American Company) Baltimore, Maryland.  v1,
    1892+
        GAU 18-22
        Nc
        NcAsbC
        NcBoA MF
        NcCJ
        NcCoB
        NcD
        NcDur
        NcDurC 58
        NcElcU
        NcFayC
        NcFayS
        NcFB
        NcGrS
        NcHY
        NcRR 75
        NcRo

(AFRO-AMERICAN.)
   NcRS
   NcRSA
   NcRSH
   NcSalL
   NcWS
   ScCOB
   ScOrC
   ScOrS 1949-58 MF
   ScU
   TNMe MF
   TNF
   VFeC
   VFsR
   VHaI
   VHfB
   VNsC
   VRpL
   VStC
   VStL
   VUnR
   VUnU
   VUnV
   VUtS

AFRO-AMERICAN STUDIES.
  (Science Publishers, Inc.) New York. 1970+
   NcElcU 1+
   NcRS 1+
   ScCOB
   VCoU 2+
   VUnV 1+

AFRO-AMERICAN WORLD.
   GAU 1

AFRO-ASIAN THEATRE BULLETIN.
  (American Educational Theatre Association) Lawrence,
  Kansas. v1-5, no2, 0 1965-1970//
   ScCLEA 1-5

AGRICULTURAL AND MECHANICAL NORMAL COLLEGE INFORMER.
    Pine Bluff, Arkansas.  vl, Ag 1940+
       TNF (1-2)

AJAX; INTERNATIONAL MONTHLY MAGAZINE OF POETRY, LITERA-
TURE AND ART.
    St. Louis, Missouri.  1916
       TNF (34), (35)

AKWESASNE NOTES.
    (Native American) Middletown, Connecticut.  1969
       TRR

ALABAMA ENTERPRISE.
       A-AR

ALABAMA GUIDE.
       A-AR

ALABAMA STATE TEACHER'S JOURNAL.
    Huntsville, Alabama.  1885+
       TNF (5-8)

ALABAMA TRIBUNE.
       A-AR

ALBION.
    New York.  Je 22, 1822-Ja 30, 1875//
       ATT (8-10)
       VHaI (8-10)
       VUnU (8-10)

ALEXANDER'S MAGAZINE.
    Boston.  1-7, My 1905-Ap 1909//
       AAM 1-7
       GA 1-7 MF
       GAU 5
       TNF 1-7
       VHaI (1, 5)

AMERICAN-ANTI SLAVERY ALMANAC.
Boston; New York.  1836-47//?
TNF 1-4

AMERICAN ANTI-SLAVERY REPORTER.
(American Anti-Slavery Society) New York.  vl,
no1-8, Ja-Ag 1834//  (Supersedes:  Anti-Slavery
Reporter (Je-N 1833))
GA 1 MF
ScU 1
VHaI 1

AMERICAN BANNER.
Bay Minette, Alabama.
A-AR (1-3)

AMERICAN BAPTIST.
GAU (57), (70)

AMERICAN COUNCIL REPORT ON RACE RELATIONS.
Chicago.  vl, 1948+
TNF (1-5)

AMERICAN CRITERION.
New York.  vl, no1-3, O 1935-Ja 1936//
TNF (1)

AMERICAN FREEDMAN.
(American Freedmen's Union Commission) New York.
1-3, Ap 1866-Jl 1869//
TNF (1-2)

AMERICAN HOME MISSIONARY.
(ACMS) Cincinnati, Ohio.  1-24, 1895-1918//
TNDC (1-24)

AMERICAN JUBILEE.
New York.  vl, no1-12, Mr 1854-Ap 1855//  (Super-
seded by Radical Abolitionist)
GA 1 MF
VHaI 1
VNsC 1

AMERICAN LIFE.
Chicago. vl, 1926+
TNF

AMERICAN MAGAZINE.
New York. 1, My 1905+
ScCLP (65-71, 98, 106-111)-(113)-(115-122)-(124-137)-(139-147)-(149)-(152-153)-(156-157)-(159)-(162)
ScGRVF 62-65, 71-77

AMERICAN MISSIONARY.
(American Missionary Association) New York. 1-10, 1846-56; (s2) vl-20, 1857-76; ns vl, 1877; v32-88, no3, 1878-My 1934// 63-82 also as ns vl-20, 1929-34 issued as fourth no. each month of Congregationalist. Volume numbering irregular. Merged into Missionary Herald.
VHaI s2 vl-(15-20, 40-80)

AMERICAN MUSEUM: OR ANNUAL REGISTER OF FUGITIVE PIECES, ANCIENT AND MODERN.
Philadelphia. 1978// Also called vl3 of American Museum of Universal Magazine
ScGRVF 1

AMERICAN NEGRO REFERENCE GUIDE.
ATT 1

AMERICAN TEACHER'S ASSOCIATION BULLETIN.
(ATA) Atlanta, Georgia. vl6, 1938-v38 1966//
GAU 57-58, 60-64
VHaI (16-18), (20-24), (26), (28-29), 36-38

AMERICAN UNITY.
(Council Against Intolerance in America) New York. 1, O 1942+
GAU 2
VHaI (1-7)-(9)-15
VUnV (1)-2, (4)-6-(7)-(19)

AMERICAN WOODSMAN.
      TNF 1

AMISTAD.
      Atlanta, Georgia; Worcester, Massachusetts.  D 1937+
         TNF (1-11)

AMSTERDAM NEWS.
    New York.  1, 1909+
         NcCoB
         NcD 9, 16, 72+, (64), MF 65+
         NcDurC (43)+
         NcElcU
         NcRR 59-60
         NcRSH
         VHaI
         VNsC
         VStC
         VUnV 57-60, 63+

ANGLO-AFRICAN MAGAZINE.
    New York.  v1-2, no3, Ja 1859-Mr 1860//
         ATT 1-12
         GAU 1-12
         NcBoA
         ScCoC 1
         VcwM 1
         VHaI (1)-2
         VMaC 1
         VUnU 1-2 MF
         VUnV 1

ANGLO-AMERICAN MAGAZINE.
    Toronto.  1-7, Jl 1852-D 1855//
         ScGRVF 2

ANTI-SLAVERY ADVOCATE.
    London.  v1-3, no5, O 1852-My 1863//
         VHaI (2)

ANTI-SLAVERY EXAMINER.
   (American Anti-Slavery Society) New York.   no1-14,
   1836-45//
      GA 1-14 MF
      ScU 1-14
      VHaI 2, 5, 6, 11-12, 14
      VNsC 1-14

ANTI-SLAVERY MONTHLY REPORTER.
   London.   v1-6, no8, Je 1825-J1 1836//
      TNF (2)
      VHaI (1)

ANTI-SLAVERY RECORD.
   (American Anti-Slavery Society) New York.   1-3,
   Ja 1835-D 1837//
      GA 1-3 MF
      ScU 1-3 MF
      VHaI 1-3
      VMaC 1-3
      VNsC 1-3

ANTI-SLAVERY REPORTER AND ABORIGINE'S FRIEND.
   (Anti-Slavery and Aborigine's Protection Society)
   London.   1-6, Ja 15, 1840-D 24, 1845; ns v1-7, 1846-
   52; s3 v1-20, 1853-80; s4 v1-29, 1881-1909; s5 v1,
   1909+ (Supersedes British Emancipator.  Ja 15, 1840-
   D 1845 as British and Foreign Anti-Slavery Reporter;
   Ja 1846-My 1909 as Anti-Slavery Reporter)
      ATT 1-29
      TNF (1-6), (2), (24-54)
      VHaI s4, (19-20)-22; (24-29) s5 (1-3), (5-11)
       (13-16-(10-24)-27-(31-32), (34)

ANTI-SLAVERY TRACTS.
   (American Anti-Slavery Society) New York.   1-20,
   1855-56; ns1-25, 1860-61//
      GA 1 MF
      VHaI 1, 4-5, 8-11, 13, 16
      VNsC 1-20

APEX NEWS.
    Atlantic City, New Jersey.
        TNF (35-37)

APPLAUSE.
    Dallas, Texas.  vl, 1933?
        TNF

APPROACH.
    Rosewart, Pennsylvania.
        TNF

ARAB WORLD.
    New York.  1954
        TNF (10-12), 13, (14-17)

ARCHON.
    (Zeta Phi Beta) Oakland, California.  vl, 1930?
        ATT 20
        TNF (4-5), (8), (10-11), (17-18), 19, (20-21)
        VHaI (17-19)-(21-22), (25)

ARGUS.
    Albany, New York.  w 1813-94//?
        GAU Ap 15, 1876

ARKANSAS SURVEY JOURNAL.
    w?
        GAU My 17, 1952

ARTS QUARTERLY.
    (Dillard University) New Orleans, Louisiana.
    1-2 Ap/Je 1937-D 1939//
        ATT 1
        TNF (1-2)

ASHANTI PIONEER.
    Kumasi, Ghana.  1939+
        NcDurC 1-24 MF

ASSOCIATION FOR STUDY OF NEGRO LIFE AND HISTORY ANNUAL
REPORT.
  Washington, D. C. 1, 1915/17+
    TNF (55)

ASSOCIATION OF BUSINESS OFFICERS IN SCHOOLS FOR NEGROES
PROCEEDINGS.
  1, 1939+
    ScOrS 2-3, 5-6, 17-19, 21, 28

ATHENS CLIPPER.
  w? Athens, Georgia.
    GAU (4), 5-6, 8, 13, 15-16

ATLANTA DAILY WORLD.
  Atlanta, Georgia. w, sw, tw, d Ag 1928+
    ATT 1965
    GAU (D 2, 1931-D 1969) MF
    NcD 1972
    NcElcU
    NcDurC 1957+
    NcFayS 1968-F 1972; Ag 1972
    ScCOB
    ScOrC 1928+
    ScOrS
    TNF
    TNK
    VHaI +
    VNsC +
    VStC

ATLANTA INDEPENDENT.
  Atlanta, Georgia. w 1903+
    ATT Ja 23, 1904-D 29, 1928
    GAU Ja 23, 1904-D 29, 1928
    NcDurC Ja 23, 1904-D 29, 1928

ATLANTA INQUIRER.
  Atlanta, Georgia. w
    ATT
    GAU

ATLANTA POST.
    Atlanta, Georgia.   w?
      GAU My 3, 1923

ATLANTA UNIVERSITY BULLETIN.
    Atlanta, Georgia.   1883+
      ATT 85
      GASC (61)-69, 72-75
      GAU 1+
      NcElcU
      NcRR 61+
      TNF 54-(71), (72-85), (87)

ATLANTA UNIVERSITY PUBLICATION (BULLETIN).
    1, 1944+
      VHaI 24-28

ATLANTA VOICE.
    Atlanta, Georgia.
      TRR

AUGUSTA CHRONICLE AND GAZETTE OF THE STATE.
    Augusta, Georgia.   Various numbers of (v3-v6)
    1789-1794
      ScU 3-6 MF

AUGUSTA UNION.
    Augusta, Georgia.   w 1889-1904//?
      GAU Mr 11, 1889

AURORA.
    (Sigma Gamma Rho Sorority Official Organ) v15, 1947.
    Indianapolis, Indiana.   v1, 1925?
      TNF (10), (13), (14), (15), (19)
      VHaI (15)

BAGS AND BAGGAGE.
    (International Brotherhood of Red Caps) Chicago.
    1, Ag 1937+
      TNF (4-6)

BALL AND CHAIN.
   Berkeley, California.  vl, 1969+
      NcElcU
      TNF 1

BALLOUS PICTORIAL DRAWING ROOM COMPANION.
   Boston.  1-17, My 3 1851-D 24 1859//  (As Gleason's
   Pictorial Drawing Room Companion.  vl-7, My 1851-
   D 1854)
      VHaI My 1851-D 24, 1859 MF
      VUnU My 1851-D 24, 1859 MF

BANC.
   (Black, Afro-American, Negro, Colored) Nashville.
   vl, 1970+
      NcElcU
      NcRR 2+
      VHaI 1+

BANTU STUDIES.
   Johannesburg, South Africa.  vl-15, no4, O 1921-
   D 1941//
      TNJ-S 1-15

BANTU TEACHER'S JOURNAL.
   Pietermaritzburg, South Africa.  1, O 1919-35 no2,
   1956//  (Ja 1954 as Native Teacher's Journal)
      VHaI (33-35)

BANTU WORLD.
      ATT (1-5)

BAPTIST LAYMAN.
   Nashville.
      TNBPB

BAPTIST LEADER.
   Philadelphia.  1 Ap 1939+
      A-AR 1-6, 7-(10), 11-(12)-18

BAPTIST PIONEER.
      A-AR

BAPTIST TRAINING UNION INTERMEDIATE QUARTERLY.
    Nashville.
        TNBPB

BAPTIST TRAINING UNION YOUNG PEOPLE'S AND ADULT QUARTERLY.
    Nashville.
        TNBPB

BAPTIST VANGUARD.
        GAU (65)

BARRISTER.
    Washington, D. C.  v1, 1940+
        ATT 1-3

BE RECONCILED.
        TNF

BEGINNER'S QUARTERLY.
    Nashville.
        TNBPB

BELGIAN CONGO TODAY.
    Brussels.  v1-9, no2, 1952-Ap/My 1960//
        ATT 5-8
        GAU (2-3), (5), (7)-8
        TNF (7), 8, (9)
        VHaI 7-(8-9)

BETA KAPPA CHI BULLETIN.
    Nashville.  v1, 1943+
        ATT 5+
        TNF (7), (9), (13), (26-29)
        TNK

BIBLIOTHEQUE SLAVE EZEVIRIENNE.
    Paris.  no1-16, 1879-1906//
        ScU

BIM.
    St. Michael, Barbados, West Indies.  v12, 1968
        TNF 3-4
        VHaI (5)

BIRMINGHAM WORLD.
    Birmingham, Alabama.  w?
       A-AR S 17, 1940+
       ATT 1968
       S.D. Bishop +
       TNMe J2, 1948-D 1970 MF

BLACK ACADEMY REVIEW:  THE QUARTERLY OF THE BLACK WORLD.
    Buffalo, New York.  1970+
       GA 1
       NcBOA
       NcElcU 1+
       NcFayS 1+
       NcSalL
       ScCOB
       TNF (1), 2
       VCoU 2+
       VFsR 2+
       VHaI 3+

BLACK AMERICA; THE MAGAZINE THAT CREATED MISS BLACK
AMERICA.
    Philadelphia.
       NcElcU

BLACK BOOKS BULLETIN.
    (Institute of Positive Education) Chicago.  v1,
    1971+
       ATT 1+
       NcElcU
       TNF (1), 2
       VHaI 1+

BLACK BUSINESS DIGEST.
    Philadelphia.  v1, 1970+
       GA 2+
       NcDur
       NcFayC 2
       NcFayS 2
       ScCOB

(BLACK BUSINESS DIGEST.)
    TNF
    VCwM 1+
    VHaI (1) +

BLACK CAREERS.
    Philadelphia.  v5, no4, Jl/Ag 1969+  (Formerly:
    Project:  Guidelines to Equal Opportunity Employment)
        GA 8+

BLACK CHILD ADVOCATE.
    (Black Child Development Institute) Washington, D. C.
    1971?+
        NcFayS 1

BLACK COLLEGIAN.
    New Orleans, Louisiana.  1971+
        GA 1+
        NcElcU
        NcFayS 3
        ScOrS 1-2 MF
        TRR
        VHaI 1+
        VNsC 1+

BLACK COMMUNICATOR.
    (Urban Communications Group) Washington, D. C.
    1970+
        TRR

BLACK CREATION.
    (Institute of Afro-American Affairs) New York.  v1,
    1970+
        GA 3+
        NcCJ (2), (3), (4)
        NcElcU
        NcUw 2
        VHaI (1)+
        VUnV 3+

BLACK DIALOGUE.
    San Francisco; New York.  1, 1965+
        NcElcU 1+
        VCoU +

BLACK DISPATCH.
    Oklahoma City, Oklahoma.  1916+
        VHaI +
        VNsC

BLACK EMPIRE.
        TJL

BLACK ENTERPRISE.
    New York.  1970+
        AAM
        GA 1+
        NcBoA 2+
        NcBuC 1+
        NcCJ (2), (3)
        NcCoB 2
        NcCU 1+
        NcCuW 1+
        NcElcU
        NcFayS 1+
        NcGuG
        NcMip
        NcRR 2+
        NcRSA
        NcRSH
        ScCLEA 1+
        ScCOB
        ScOrS 1-2 MF
        TNF (1), (2)
        TTM
        TRR
        VBrC 1+
        VCwM 1+
        VHaI 1+
        VHsC
        VMbC 2+
        VMwC (1)+

(BLACK ENTERPRISE.)
      VNnS (2)+
      VNsC 1+
      Voorhees
      VRmW 1+
      VUnU 1+
      VVaC

BLACK HISTORY MUSEUM NEWSLETTER.
      TNF

BLACK IMAGES.
    Toronto. 1, 1972+
      GA

BLACK INFORMATION INDEX.
    Herndon, Virginia. 1970//
      GA
      NcElcU
      ScOrS
      TNF (1)
      VHaI 1+
      VUnV 1+

BLACK INK.
    (University of North Carolina) Chapel Hill, North
    Carolina.
      NcElcU

BLACK LAW JOURNAL.
    (Black World Foundation) Sausalito, California. v1,
    1971+
      ATT (1)+
      GA 2+
      TNF (1), (2)
      TRR
      VHaI 1+

BLACK LAW JOURNAL.
    (University of California) Los Angeles.
      NcElcU

BLACK LINES.
   (University of Pittsburgh) Pittsburgh, Pennsylvania.
   v1-3, no2, Fall 1970+ Winter 1972//
      NcCJ (1)
      NcElcU 1
      TNF (1), (2)
      VHaI 2+
      VUtS 1+

BLACK MAN.
   London.  v1-3, 1935-1938//?
      ATT

BLACK MAN.
   (The official organ of the African Nationalist
   Union) Kingston, Jamaica.  v1, 1969+
      ATT
      VHaI (1-3)

BLACK NEWS DIGEST.
   (U.S. Department of Labor) Washington, D. C.
      AAM 1
      NcCJ (1-3)
      NcElcU
      NcSalL 2
      ScCOB
      TNF (1-3)
      TRR
      VHaI 1+
      VUnU 2+

BLACK ORPHEUS:  JOURNAL OF AFRICAN AND AFRO-AMERICAN
LITERATURE.
   Ibadan, Nigeria.  no1-22, S 1957-1967//
      TNF (2-5), (7-11), 14
      VCwM 1-4, 6-9, 11, 13-22
      VHaI (1-2)
      VNsC (2)

BLACKOUT.
      TRR

BLACK PANTHER PARTY INTERCOMMUNAL NEWS SERVICE.
San Francisco. 1967+ (Formerly: Black Panther)
ATT 4+
NcDur
NcElcU
NcWS
TNF
TRR
VCoU 4+
VFsR 5+
VHaI (3)+
VNsC 1+
VUnV

BLACK PAPERS.
(Institute of the Black World) Atlanta, Georgia.
1, Je 16, 1969+
ScCOB

BLACK POLITICIAN.
(Urban Affairs Institute) Los Angeles. 1969+
ATT 1
NcElcU
NcSalL 3+
ScCOB
ScOrS 2+
ScRHW
ScU
TMaU 1-3
TNF (1-3)
TNK
TRR
VHaI (1)+
VMaC 1+
Voorhees
VRmW 1+

BLACK POLITICS.
Berkeley, California. 1, 1968+
NcElcU

BLACK POSITION.
    (Broadside Press) Detroit, Michigan.  no1, 1971+
        ATT
        GA

BLACK REPUBLICAN.
        ScOrS

BLACK REVIEW.
    New York.  v1, 1971+
        VCwM 1

BLACK SCHOLAR:  JOURNAL OF BLACK STUDIES AND RESEARCH.
    (Black World Foundation) Sausalito, California.
    1969+
        AAM 2
        ATT 1
        GA 1+
        NcBuC 1+
        NcCoB 3+
        NcCuW 3+
        NcElcU 1
        NcFayS 1
        NcGuG
        NcRR 3+
        NcRS 1
        NcSalL
        ScCOB
        ScOrS 1-3 MF
        ScU
        S.D. Bishop 1
        TJeCN 2
        TJoS
        TNF (1-4)
        TNK 1-14
        TNLO
        TNMe +
        TRR
        VCoU 1+
        VCwM 1+
        VGmC 1+

(BLACK SCHOLAR:   JOURNAL OF BLACK STUDIES AND RESEARCH.)
      VHaI 1+
      VKpL (3)+
      VNsC 1+
      VUnU 1+
      VUnV 1+

BLACK SHADES.
   Washington, D. C.
      NcElcU

BLACK SPORTS.
   New York.   1971+
      GA 1+
      NcDur
      NcEC
      NcElcU
      NcSalL
      TNF (1-2)
      TNK
      TNT
      VHaI 1+

BLACK STARS.
   Chicago.   v1, N 1971+
      NcCJ (2)
      NcDur
      NcEC
      NcElcU
      VHaI 1+
      VNaB 1+
      VUnV 1+
      VUsN 1+

BLACK THEATRE:   A PERIODICAL OF THE BLACK THEATRE
MOVEMENT.
   (New Lafayette Theatre) New York.   1968+   (Formerly:
   Black Theatre News)
      NcElcU
      NcFayS (3)+
      NcGuG

(BLACK THEATRE:  A PERIODICAL OF....)
        TNF
        TNK
        VCoU 4+
        VCwM (2)+

BLACK THEATRE BULLETIN.
        ScCLEA

BLACK THEATRE MAGAZINE.
    1966+
        TNF 5-6

BLACK TIMES.
    w Albany, California.  1, Ja 15, 1971+
        ATT 1+
        AU
        TNF
        TRR
        VFeC 1+
        VFsR 2+
        VHaI 1+
        VNsC
        VUnU 1+
        VUsN

BLACK WORLD.
    Chicago.  v19-25, no6, 1970-Ap 1976//  (Formerly:
    Negro Digest)
        AU +
        GA 16-19
        NcCJ (19-21)
        NcCO
        NcCoB 21+
        NcDaD 18
        NcDur
        NcElcU
        NcFayS 19
        NcHyL 19+
        NcL 21+
        NcPC
        NcSalL 20+

(BLACK WORLD.)
   ScCLEA 19+
   ScOrC 1+
   ScOrS 19-21 MF
   ScRHW 22+
   TMNH
   TN-E
   TNF (19-21)
   TNK
   TNLO
   TRR
   VBrC 19+
   VCoU 19+
   VCrR 21+
   VFsR (20)+
   VHaI 19+
   VHcC 21+
   VHoC (19-20)+
   VKpL (21)+
   VMbC 19+
   VMwC 19+
   VNsC 19+
   VRoP 19+
   VRpL (19)+
   VStC
   VUnU 19+ MF
   VUsN
   VVaC

BLANCO Y NEGRO.
  w Madrid, Spain. 1-46, 1891-Jl 12, 1936//
   NcCuW

BLESSING LETTER.
  (House of Prayer for All People) Denver, Colorado.
   TNDC (1)?

BONGO MAN.
  no1, D 1968+
   ATT 1+

BOOKMARK.
   (Tuskegee Library Publications) Tuskegee, Alabama.
   v1, 1934+?
     ATT 1-13

BOOKS FOR AFRICA.
   (International Committee on Christian Literature for
   Africa) London.  1, 1931+
     TNJ-S 1-9, 14-15, (16), (17-18), 25-33
     TNF (1), (2), (7), 8, (9), 10-13, (14), 15, (16),
     17-19, (20-24)

BOSTON CHRONICLE.
   w Boston.  1915+
     GAU 34

BOULE JOURNAL.
   Wilberforce, Ohio.
     TNF

BROADCASTER.
   Nashville.  1, 1928+
     TNF (1-3), (5-7), 8-10, (11), 12-13, (14-15),
     (19-20), (22-23) 31

BROADAX.
   w Chicago.  1895-1919//?
     VStC

BROAD AXE.
   w S 17, 1891-Je 11, 1903//
     GAU MF

BROADSIDE.
     ATT

BRONZE CITIZEN.
   Peoria, Illinois.  v1, 1946+
     ATT 1

BRONZEMAN.
    Harrisburg, Pennsylvania.
      TNF

BROWN AMERICAN.
    (Bureau On Negro Affairs) Philadelphia.  1, Ap 1936+
      ATT (1-8)
      GA 1-10 MF
      TNF (1-4, 5, (6-10)
      VHaI 1-5
      VNsC (1-5)

BROWNIE'S BOOK.
    New York.  1-2, 1920-21//
      ATT 1-2
      GAU 1-2
      TNF 1
      VHaI 1-2 MF
      VUnU 1-2 MF

BUSINESS LEAGUE BULLETIN.
      ATT 1-3

C. I. A. A. BULLETIN.
    (Colored Intercollegiate Athletic Association)
    Norfolk, Virginia.  1912+
      TNF 22, 24, 25, 28-38, 41-43
      VHaI 28-29, 31, 35-36, 37, 40-42

CALHOUN COLORED SCHOOL REPORTS.
    Calhoun, Alabama
      ATT

CALIFORNIA EAGLE.
    w Los Angeles.  Mr 8, 1879+
      ATT

CALIFORNIA VOICE.
    w Oakland, California.  1919+
      GAU D 28, 1951

CALL AND POST (CLEVELAND).
  w F 22, 1921+   (1921-29? as Cleveland Call)
      GAU 1961-1964
      NcCJ
      NcD S 30, 1972+
      NcRR 1967
      TNF

CAPE FEAR MERCURY.
  (Early State Records Series) Wilmington, North
  Carolina.
      ScU MF

CARAVAN.
  New York.  vl, 1923+
      NcCJ
      NcElcU
      NcRR

CARIBBEAN.
  (University of the West Indies) Kingston, Jamaica.
  1949+
      TNF (1), 2, 4, (6-9), (13)

CARIBBEAN COMMISSION.
      TNF

CARIBBEAN HISTORICAL REVIEW.
  (Historical Society of Trinidad and Tobago) Port of
  Spain, Trinidad.  1, D 1950+
      TNF

CAROLINA PEACEMAKER.
  Greensboro, North Carolina.  1967+
      NcD
      NcDurC
      NcGuG

CAROLINA TIMES.
  Durham, North Carolina.  1925+
      NcCoB
      NcDur

(CAROLINA TIMES.)
      NcDurC 1949
      NcEC
      NcElcU
      NcFayC
      NcFayS 1967
      NcRR 1967+
      NcRSA
      NcSalL
      ScCOB
      ScOrC 1919
      TNF

CAROLINIAN.
    Raleigh, North Carolina.  w 1941+
      NcCJ
      NcDurC Ap 1952
      NcElcU
      NcFayS 1967+
      NcRR 1945+
      NcRSA
      NcSalL

CENTER.
    Atlanta, Georgia.  v1, 1960+
      TNF

CENTRAL AFRICA STORY.
    (Central Africa Mission, Churches of Christ)
      TNDC 1+

CENTRAL AFRICA POST.
    Lusaka, Rhodesia.
      NcDurC Ja 1, 1960-F 28, 1964 MF

CENTRE DE RECHERCHE ET D'INFORMATION SOCIO-POLITIQUES.
ETUDES AFRICAINES.
    Brussels.  1960+
      NcGU

CHAMPION MAGAZINE.
    Chicago.  1, 1916/17+
        ATT 1
        TNF (1)

CHARLOTTE POST.
    Charlotte, North Carolina.
        GAU Mr 27, 1952

CHICAGO BEE.
    w Chicago.  1909-31//?
        GAU

CHICAGO DEFENDER.
    w Chicago.  1905+
        ATT Ap 2, 1921+
        AU +
        GAU 1909-1916+
        NcCoB
        NcD
        NcDurC Ja 1949+ MF 1921+
        NcFayS 1969+
        NcMiP
        NcRR
        NcRSA
        NcSalL
        NcWS
        S.D. Bishop+
        ScCOB
        ScOrS 1971+
        ScU (1921-1967) MF
        TNF
        TN-H
        TNK
        VHaI +; MF 1947+
        VUnU 1971+
        VStC 1947+ MF

CHRISTIAN ECHO.
        TnMH+

CHRISTIAN EXAMINER.
    Boston.  1-87, 1824-N 1869//
        TNF (29)

CHRISTIAN INFORMER.
    (Mississippi Christian Missionary Convention)
    Edwards, Mississippi
        TNDC

CHRISTIAN INSTITUTE MESSENGER.
    Winston-Salem, North Carolina
        TNDC

CHRISTIAN MESSENGER.
    (Jamaica Mission, UCMS:   Texas Christian Missionary
    Society) Dallas, Texas
        TNDC

CHRISTIAN OUTLOOK.
    Chicago.
        TNDC

CHRISTIAN PLEA.
    (NCMC) Columbus, Ohio.  1, 1899?+
        TNDC (1-65)

CHRISTIAN RECORDER.
    (African Methodist Episcopal Church) Philadelphia.
    1 1852+
        GAU My 19, 1892, Mr 17, 1898, 1901/02, Ap 23, 1936
        TN

CHRISTIAN STANDARD.
    w Cincinnati, Ohio.   1866+
        TNDC 1+

CHRONICLE.
    (Federation of Rhodesia and Nyasaland) Lusaka,
    Rhodesia.  1894+
        NcDurC 67-71
        TNF (37-39)

CHRONICLE.
    South Carolina.
      NcD


CITIZEN.
    Boston.  v1, 1915+
      GAU S 1915


CIVIL RIGHTS DIGEST.
    (U.S. Commission on Civil Rights) Washington, D. C.
    v1, 1967+
      GA 5+
      NcElcU 1+
      NcRSA
      NcUW 1
      ScCOB
      ScGRAVF
      ScRHW
      TJoS
      TNF
      TNLO
      VFsR 4+
      VGmC 1-4
      VHaI 1-(2)+
      VHoC (1)-(3)
      VHsC (2)+
      VKpL 1+
      VMaC 1+
      VRmW 1+
      VUtS (3)+


CLEVELAND GAZETTE.
    Cleveland, Ohio.  w Ag 25, 1883+
      GAU Ag 25, 1883-My 20, 1945


COLD TRUTH.
    New York.
      NcElcU


COLLEGE DREAMER.
    1922
      ATT 1

COLLEGE LANGUAGE ASSOCIATION (CLA BULLETIN).
    Fort Valley, Georgia.  1-7, 19. 1934-51//
        VHaI (11)


COLLEGE LANGUAGE ASSOCIATION JOURNAL.
    Baltimore, Maryland.  vl, N 1957+
        ATT 1
        GA 1
        GAMB (2-3), (4-5), 10, 11, 12
        GASC
        NcDurC 1
        NcElcU 1
        NcFayS 1
        NcMip 13+
        NcSalL 1
        ScCOB 12-
        ScOrC (7-8)-10, (12)
        ScOrS 3-5, 7-9, 10
        TNF (1), (4-13)
        VCwM 10+
        VHaI 1+
        VMbC 13+


COLONIZATION HERALD AND GENERAL REGISTER.
    (Philadelphia Colonization Society) Philadelphia.
    1-3(no1-67), Ap 4, 1835-Mr 1845; ns no1-6 Ja-Je 1839;
    (s3) vl-1, Ja 3-5 27, 1843; (s4) no1-18, O 1843-
    Mr 1845; (55) no1-45, Ap 1845-D 1848; (s6) no1-152,
    Jl 1850-Ja-Mr 1868//?
        TNF


COLONIZATIONIST AND JOURNAL OF FREEDOM.
    Boston.  Ap 1833-Ap 1834//
        TNF 1


COLOR.
    Charleston, West Virginia.  1, 1944+
        ATT (9-11)
        NcRR
        TNF
        VStC

COLOR LINE; A MONTHLY ROUND-UP OF THE FACTS OF NEGRO
AMERICAN PROGRESS AND OF THE GROWTH OF AMERICAN DEMOCRACY.
    Mt. Vernon, New York.  v1-2, no6, Jl/Ag 1946-Jl/Ag
    1947//
        GA 1-2 MF
        VNsC (1-2)

COLORED ALABAMIAN.
    Montgomery, Alabama.  1-10, 1907-16//
        A-AR (1-6), 7-(8-10)

COLORED AMERICAN.
    w New York.  Ja 7, 1837.  (As Weekly Advocate.  Ja-
    F 1837)
        ATT Mr 14, 1840-Mr 13, 1841
        GAMB Ja 7-F 25, 1837, Mr 14, 1840-Mr 13, 1841 MF
        GAU Ja 7, 1837-N 12, 1904
        TNF 1900-1909
        VHaI 1837-39; MF 1840-41+
        VstC
        VUnU 1840-41 MF

COLORED AMERICAN MAGAZINE.
    New York.  v1-17, no5 My 1900-N 1909//
        ATT 1-2
        GA 1-17 MF
        NcCuW
        ScU 1-17
        VHaI (1)-(4-7)-(14)-(17)

COLORED AMERICAN REVIEW.
    New York.  v1, 1915+
        TNF

COLORED BASEBALL AND SPORTS.
    1934
        ATT 1

COLORED CITIZEN.
    A-AR Ap 5-My 17, 1884

COLORED EMBALMER.
   Chicago.  v1, 1927+
      ATT 1-4
      TNF (6-8)

COLORED HERALD.
      GAU 1915

COLORED MORTICIANS' BULLETIN.
      ATT 3

COLORED SERVANT GIRL.
   1910
      ATT 1

COLORED TEACHER.
   m New Orleans, Louisiana.  v1, 1906?
      ATT (12-14)
      VHaI (1)

COLUMBIAN.
   w Chicago.  1906+
      GAU 1911

COLUMBIAN CENTINEL.
   Boston.
      ScCSM D 2, 1797

COLUMBIAN MAGAZINE; OR, MONTHLY MISCELLANY.
   Kingston, Jamaica
      TNF (2)

COLUMBUS WORLD.
      GAU 1952

COLUMNS.
   (Hampton Institute) Hampton, Virginia.  v1, no1,
   Ap 1955+
      VHaI

COMMON GROUND.
    (Common Council for American Unity) New York.  1,
    S 1940+
        TNF (10)
        VStC

COMMON SENSE HISTORICAL REVIEW.
    Chicago.  vl, 1949
        TNF

COMMUNITIES IN ACTION.
    Washington, D. C.  vl, 1966+
        TNF

COMMUNITY.
    Chicago.  1940+  (Formerly:  The Catholic
    Interracialist)
        GAU (13), (15-19), (21-22)
        NcCU 23+
        NcDurC
        TNF (15-27)
        VcoU 30+

COMPASS.
    (Elizabeth City State University) Elizabeth City,
    North Carolina.  vl, 1940?
        NcElcU

COMPETITOR.
    Pittsburgh, Pennsylvania.  vl-3, no4, 1920-21//
        AAM 1-3
        GA 1-3 MF

CONGO; REVUE GENERALE DE LA COLONIE BELGE.
    Brussels.  1, 1920+
        TNJ-S 1-17, (18), 19-20, (21)

CONGO CHRISTIAN.
        TNDC

CONGO CHURCH NEWS.
   TNJ-S 48, 54-57, 61, 64-78, 80, 83-109, 111-128,
   130-133, 170, 176, 181, 183-191, 203-

CONGO COBWEBS.
   TNDC

CONGO FIELD NEWS.
  (United Christian Missionary Society) Indianapolis.
   TNDC

CONGO MAGAZINE.
  Kinshasa, Congo.
   TNJ-S

CONGO MISSION NEWS.
  (Congo Protestant Council) Leopoldville, Congo.
  no1, 1913+
   TNDC (11-54)

CONGO NEWS LETTER.
  Sona Bata, Congo Belge. 1 Jl, 1910+
   TNDC 31-35
   VHaI (13)

CONGRESS OF RACIAL EQUALITY BULLETIN.
  New York.
   ATT

CONNECTION.
  Pittsburgh, Pennsylvania.
   NcElcU

CONSERVATOR.
  Philadelphia. v1-13, no4, 1890-Je 1919//
   ATT (1-9)
   GAU 1-30
   VHaI (1-10) MF
   VRmW 1-30
   VUnU (1-10) MF

CONTACT.
    New York.  v1, 1968+
        NcElcU
        ScSpW 1+
        TNF

CORE-LATER.
    (Congress of Racial Equality) New York.
        VHaI

CORONA.
    London.  v1, 1953+
        TNF

CRAFTSMEN AREO NEWS.
    Los Angeles.  v1-2, no5, Ja 1937-Ag 1938//?
        ATT 1-2
        TNF (1-2)

CREOLE MAGAZINE.
    New Orleans, Louisiana.  v1-2, no1, My 1899-
    Je 1900//?
        TNF (1-2)

CRESCENT.
    (Official Organ of the Phi Beta Sigma Fraternity,
    Inc.) Little Rock, Arkansas.  1921+
        ATT 3
        TNF (3), (6), (7), (11), (22), (26), (29-31), 44
        VHaI 23, 29-33

CRICKET.
    Newark, New Jersey.
        GA 1
        NcElcU

CRISIS:  A RECORD OF THE DARKER RACES.
    (National Association for the Advancement of Colored
    People) New York.  1, N 1910+
        AAM
        ATT
        GA 1-78, 1-47 MF

(CRISIS: A RECORD OF THE DARKER RACES.)
        GAMB (1-75)
        GASC 1947+
        GAU (1-27), 31, (33-35), (37-43), (45-52), (54-
          60), (62-74) MF 28-30, 32, 36, 44, 53, 61, 75
        NcBoC 1+ MF
        NcCJ 1-75 MF 76+
        NcCO
        NcCoB 37-67, 74+
        NcCU 1-76 MF
        NcDaD 1-67
        NcDur
        NcDurC 1-48
        NcElcU 1
        NcFayC 63-79
        NcFayS 38
        NcFB
        NcGU
        NcRR 43, 47, 64
        NcRS 1+
        NcRSA
        NcRSH 38
        NcSalL
        ScCOB 1-47, (53, 58-59, 62, 65-75)
        ScCOC 57
        ScCLP (54)-(56-58)-(62-65)-(67)-(75)+
        ScOrC (41-43), 46, 48, 52-56, 68-75+  1-75 MF
        ScOrS 3-34, 37-52, 58-59, 61, 63, 65, 1-76 MF
        TMU 1-47
        TNBK 68+
        TND
        TNF 1-80
        TN-H
        TNJ-S 43-56, 59-67, (68), 69-71, (72-75), 76+
        TNK
        TNL MF
        TNLO
        TNMe 1+
        TRR
        VCwM 1-67, 75+
        VFsR 79+

(CRISIS:  A RECORD OF THE DARKER RACES.)
      VHaI  (1)-(18)+ MF 1+
      VHoC  1-76 MF
      VKpL  75
      VMwC  61+
      VNnP
      VNsC  47+
      Voorhees
      VRmW
      VRoP  77+
      VRpL  (30-35)-52, 54-(65)-(71-73)+
      VStC
      VUnU  2+

CRITERION:  A QUARTERLY REVIEW.
   London.  v1-18, no2 (no1-71), O 1922-Ja 1939//
   (v4-5, no1, Ja 1926-Ja 1927 as New Criterion; v5,
   no2-v7 (no3, F 1927-Mr 1928 as Monthly Criterion)
      ScGRVF 1-18

CROSS AND THE FLAG.
   Detroit, Michigan.  1, Ap 1942+
      TNDC

CRUSADER.
   w Monroe, North Carolina.  1959?  (v9-? published in
   exile) 1967+
      ATT
      VHaI (2-3), (9-10)

CURRENT BIBLIOGRAPHY ON AFRICAN AFFAIRS.
   Westport, Connecticut.  1962+
      ScCOB
      ScRHW 1-2
      TNJ-S 1, (2-3)+
      VCwM 1, 3+
      VNsC 7+

CURRENT NEWS FROM AND ABOUT BIAFRA.
   (American Committee to Keep Biafra Alive, Inc.)
   New York
      TNJ-S

DAILY EXPRESS.
    Lagos, Nigeria.  v1, 1960+
        GAU 3
        NcDurC 1-9

DAILY SERVICE.
    Lagos, Nigeria.  1950+
        NcDurC (1) MF

DAY BOOK.
    New York.
        ATT 3-(9)
        VHaI 1-(9)
        VUnU 3-(9)

DAYTON FORUM.
    w Dayton, Ohio.  My 16, 1913+
        GAU 1941

DEFENDER.
        ScCoC (38-39), 40, (41), 42+

DELTA.
    (Delta Sigma Theta Sorority) Washington, D. C.
    v4, 1924+
        ATT 4
        VHaI 17-18, (20)

DISCIPLE HERALD.
        TNDC

DOLLAR MARK.
        ATT 1

DOUGLASS' MONTHLY.
    Rochester, New York.  v1-5, 1858-1863//
        AAM 1-5
        GA 1-5 MF
        TNF 1-5
        VHaI 1-5

DRAMATIKA:  THE MAGAZINE OF SHORT PLAYS.
    University, Alabama.  1968+
       TNF

DRUM.
       NcRR
       TNF

DUNBAR NEWS.
    New York.  1-6, My 1929-34//
       TNF (2-3)

DUNBAR RECORD.
       TNF

DYNAMITE.
    1937?
       ATT 2

EAST AFRICA AND RHODESIA.
    London.  1, S 1924+  (1924-S 3, 1936 as East Africa)
       TNF (20), 21-30, (31)
       VNsC

EAST AFRICA JOURNAL.
    Nairobi, Kenya.  1964+
       TNF
       TNMe 2+
       VHaI 8+
       VNsC 6+
       VRmW (6-7)

EAST AFRICAN AGRICULTURAL AND FORESTRY JOURNAL.
    Nairobi, Kenya.  1935+
       TNF (10-12), 15 (16)

EAST AFRICAN FORTNIGHTLY NEWS.
       VNsC

EAST AFRICAN GEOGRAPHICAL REVIEW.
    (Uganda Geographical Association) Kampala, Uganda.
    v1, Ap 1963+
       TNMe +

EAST AFRICAN STANDARD.
    Kenya, Niarobi.  1905+
       ATT 66
       NcDurC 58+

EASTERN AFRICA ECONOMIC REVIEW.
    Nairobi, Kenya.  1954+  (Formerly:  East African
    Economic Review)
       TNMe 11
       VNsC

EBONY.
    Chicago.  1, N 1945+
       AAM 1+
       ATT 1+
       AU 20+
       GA 5+, 1-20 MF
       GAU 1+
       NcALB
       NcAsbC
       NcBE 24
       NcBoA MF
       NcCJ 1-23
       NcCO 19
       NcCoB 1+
       NcCQ
       NcCuW 24+
       NcDaD 22
       NcDur
       NcDurC 1
       NcElcU 7
       NcET
       NcFayC 18-27
       NcFayS 2
       NcFB
       NcGO
       NcGrS
       NcGU 17
       NcGuG
       NcHY
       NcL

(EBONY.)

   NcLK
   NcMiP
   NcMV
   NcPC
   NcRM
   NcRR 2+
   NcRS 1+
   NcRSA 2+
   NcRSH
   NcSalC 24+
   NcSalL 20
   NcWS
   NcY
   S.D. Bishop 19-20+
   ScCLEA 24+
   ScCLP (18)-(20)-22
   ScCOB 16
   ScCoC 1-21 MF
   ScCorC (20-24)+
   ScDWE (22)+
   ScOrC 21+
   ScOrS 23-25, 30-44, 52 MF
   ScRHW 22+
   ScU
   TD 16+ MF
   TG
   TJeCN
   TJL
   TJoS
   TK
   TKM
   TLC
   TMeVH
   TMH
   TMMH
   TMMU
   TMNH
   TMS
   TM-SW 23
   TNB

(EBONY.)

TND
TND-E 26-28
TNF
TN-GH
TNJ 17+
TNJ-S (20-21, 23), 24
TNK
TNL 1-26
TNLO
TNMa 24+
TNMe 1+ MF
TNMH
TNMO 20-26
TNT
TNVH
TNW
TOR
TPM
TS-M
TTM
TWOH
VBgR
VBpL (25)+
VBrC 22+
VBrP
VCeV
VChT 20+ MF 16+
VClV
VCoU 25+
VCpL 17+
VCrR 24+
VCvC 27+, MF 24-26
VCwM 24+
VDcC 25+
VDpL 25+
VFcL
VFeC 24+
VFgM
VFpH
VFpR

(EBONY.)

    VFrB 24+
    VFsP
    VFsR 26+, MF 1-26
    VFwW 22+
    VHaI 1+
    VHcC 26+ MF, 16-25
    VHcS
    VHfB
    VHoC (25-26)+
    VHsC
    VKpL 10+
    VLaF
    VLpL 24+
    VMaC (24)+
    VMbC 24+
    VMcV (24-26)
    VMmL (21)+
    VMpL
    VMwC 8+
    VNaB
    VNnP
    VNsC 3+
    Voorhees
    VPhC 25+
    VPuL
    VPwC (24)+
    VRbC (24)-26
    VRcP (21)+
    VRmW 22+
    VRoP (26)+
    VRpL (17-23)+
    VSbC (17)+
    VSpL (21)+
    VSrL
    VSsH
    VStC
    VSUC 20+
    VTnC 21-26
    VUnR
    VUnV (3-7), (12-20), 1+

(EBONY.)
      VUrS (23-24)+
      VUsN
      VVaC
      VWcC
      VWpL

ECHO.
    Mt. Hope, West Virginia.
      GAU 1941

EDUCATION: A JOURNAL OF REPUTATION.
    (Negro Needs Society) Corona, L. I., New York.
    v1-2, no3, Ap 1935-J1/Ag 1936//?
      GA
      VHaI 1-(2)
      VUnV 1-2

EDUCATOR.
    Baltimore, Maryland. 1-2, O 1886-S 1888//
      ATT 3

EKIM'EA NSANGO.
    Bolenge, Congo.
      TNDC (1-43)?

ELEVATOR.
    w San Francisco. Ap 6, 1865+
      NcElcU (1865-1898)

EMANCIPATOR.
    1939?
      ATT 14
      GAU (5), (7-12), (14-15)

EMANCIPATOR.
    Milwaukee, Wisconsin. v1, no1-29, Ja 13-S 8, 1877//?
      ATT (1)
      VHaI (1)
      VUnU (1)

EMANCIPATOR (Complete).
     ...a reprint of the Emancipator to which are added
     a biographical sketch of Elihu Embree...
     Jonesborough, Tennessee.  vl, nol-7, Ap 30-0 31,
     1820//
          VUnV 1

EQUAL OPPORTUNITY.
     New York.  1970+
          GA 1
          NcCJ 1

ESSENCE.
     New York.  1970+
          GA 1
          NcCJ (2-3)
          NcCo 3
          NcCoB 1+
          NcDur
          NcEC
          NcElcU
          NcFayS 2
          NcL 3
          NcRR 1
          NcRSH
          TMNH
          TNF
          TNK
          TRR
          VCoU (1)+
          VCrR 2+
          VFsR 2+
          VHaI (1)+
          VKpL (2)+
          VMwC (1)+
          VUnU (1)+

ETHIOPIAN HERALD.
          ATT

EVENING APPEAL.
     F 21, 1887
          A-AR

EVERYBODY.
Omaha, Nebraska.  1958+
ATT 11+

EX UMBRA; THE MAGAZINE OF THE ARTS.
Durham, North Carolina.
VHaI (3-4), (7-8)

EXPANDING OPPORTUNITIES.
(Committee on Equality of Educational Opportunity)
v1-2, 1964-65//
NcElcU 1-2

EXPECTED.
(Official publication of the Virginia Baptist State
Convention.  Virginia Theological Seminary and
College) Lynchburg, Virginia.
TNF (30-31), (33), 34-36
VHaI (26-29), (32-33)-(38)

EXPLORATIONS IN EDUCATION.
(South Carolina State College) Orangeburg, South
Carolina.  1, Spring 1964+
VUnU (1-2), (4)-5

EYES.
Iowa City, Iowa.  v1, 1-5, Ap 1946-Je 1947
TNF

FACT SHEET.
TNF

FACTS FOR THE PEOPLE.
Washington, D. C.  v1, Je 1853-My 1854; ns v1,
no1-12, My 1855-Ap 1856//
TNF ns v1

FACTS ON FILM.
(Southern Education Reporting Service) Nashville.
no1, 1954+
AAM MF

FACULTY RESEARCH JOURNAL.
    (St. Augustine's College) Raleigh, North Carolina.
    vl, 1963+
        VHaI (2), (4-6)

FAIRVIEW SONA-TIMES.
    Detroit, Michigan.  vl, 1933+
        TNF

FEDERAL COUNCIL BULLETIN.
    (Federal Council of the Churches of Christ in
    America) New York. 1, 1918+
        TNF (23-24), (26-27), (30-31)

FEDERAL NIGERIA.
    (Federal Ministry of Information of Nigeria) Lagos,
    Nigeria. 1958
        TNF 1-2, (3-10)
        VHaI (7-9), (11)

FELLOWSHIP.
    (Fellowship of Reconciliation) New York.  1, Mr 1935+
        TNF (28-29)

FIRE:  A QUARTERLY DEVOTED TO THE YOUNGER NEGRO ARTISTS.
    New York.  vl, nol, N 1926
        GA 1 MF
        TNF
        VHaI 1
        VNsC 1

FISK HERALD.
    Nashville.  vl, 1887+
        TNF 1-2, 4-5, 12-22, 25-29, 38-45, 48-74, 76-78

FISK UNIVERSITY ANNUAL CATALOGUE.
    Nashville.  1867+
        TNF 1+

FISK UNIVERSITY.  THE CLARION.
    Nashville.
        TNF 9, 11

FISK UNIVERSITY NEWS.
    (University Alumni Association) Nashville.  vl,
    1927+
        ATT
        TNF (1-41)
        VUnV (7), (13-15)

FLAMINGO:  AFRICA'S LIVELY FAMILY MAGAZINE.
    London.  1962+
        TNF (1-4)

FLASH:  NEWSPICTURE MAGAZINE.
    Washington, D. C.  1-3, (no1-82) Mr 6, 1937-
    Ag 31, 1939//
        ATT 1-2
        TNF (1-3)

FORUM.
    1886-1950//
        NcElcU
        ScCLP 71-(98-102)-103
        ScDWE 104-112
        ScGRVF 23, 35-47, 72-103
        ScHaC 41-54, 81-(83), 84-103
        ScSPC 18-27, 76-103, 105-112
        ScSpW 1-103

FORUM QUARTERLY.
        TNF

FOUNDATION.
    Atlanta, Georgia.  1, 1911+
        ATT 9
        TNF (16), 18, (19-29), (32-42)

FOUNDATIONS; A BAPTIST JOURNAL OF HISTORY AND THEOLOGY.
    Rochester, New York.  1958.  (Supersedes Chronicle)
        ScGRVF 1+

FREE.
        GA

FREE AND ACCEPTED MASONS.
  TNF

FREE HOUSE.
  TNF

FREE LANCE; A MAGAZINE OF POETRY AND PROSE.
 Cleveland, Ohio. vl, 1953+
  TNF (2-3), (6-7), (9), (13), (15)

FREE STATE ADVOCATE.
 Mochochonono Maseru, Basutoland.
  ATT

FREEDMEN'S RECORD.
 (New England Freedmen's Aid Society) Boston. vl-5,
 noll, Ja 1865-Ap 1874// (1 as Freedmen's Journal)
  TNF 1-4

FREEDOM.
  TNF

FREEDOM'S JOURNAL.
 New York. 1-2 (nol-104) Mr 1827-Mr 28, 1829//
  ATT 1-2 MF
  GAMB 1-2
  GAU 1-2
  NcCuW 1-2
  VHaI 1-2 MF
  VUnU 1-2 MF

FREEDOMWAYS: A QUARTERLY REVIEW OF THE FREEDOM MOVEMENT.
 New York. vl, 1961+
  AAM 3, 6-7
  ATT 1+
  AU +
  GA 11+
  GAU (1-7)
  NcCoB 1+
  NcDurC 3+
  NcElcU 1+
  NcFayS 8

(FREEDOMWAYS:  A QUARTERLY REVIEW...)
        NcGrE 1-2 MF 5+
        NcGU 1+
        NcRR
        NcRS 1+
        NcRSA
        NcRSH
        NcSalL 1-5 MF, 5+
        ScCOB
        ScOrC 3-5 (7-8)+
        ScOrS 4, MF 5-9, 11, 13
        TNF 1, (2), 3-5, 6, 7, 8
        TNLO
        TNMe 1+
        TRR
        VCwM 1+
        VFeC 10+
        VFpH
        VFsR 11+, MF 1-10
        VHaI 1-(9)+
        VUnU 3+

FREEHOLDER'S JOURNAL.
    London.  no1-76, Ja 31, 1721-My 18, 1723//
        ATT 1-76 MF
        GAU 1-76
        VHaI 1-76 MF

FREEING THE SPIRIT:  THE MAGAZINE OF BLACK LITURGY.
    (National Office for Black Catholics) Washington,
        D. C.  v1, Ag 1971+
        TNF

FREEMAN.
    w Indianapolis, Indiana.  1884-1926//?
        GAU 1910

FREEMAN; A JOURNAL OF IDEAS ON LIBERTY.
    Irvington-on-Hudson, New York.  1950+
        ScGRVF 14+
        ScOrS
        VBrC 13-19

(FREEMAN; A JOURNAL OF IDEAS ON LIBERTY.)
     VCnC 15+
     VRpL (10-12)+
     VUtS (2)-(16-17)

FRIEND OF AFRICA.
   (Society for the Extinction of the Slave Trade, and
   for the Civilization of Africa) v1-3 (no1-28)
   Ja 1, 1841-F 1843// (Supersedes: Friend of the
   Africans)
     TNF 1-3

GENEVE AFRIQUE/ACTA AFRICANA.
   Carouge-Geneve, Switzerland. 1962+
     TNJ-S 3+

GHANA DAILY GRAPHIC.
     ATT

GHANA EVENING NEWS.
   Accra, Ghana. 1954+
     NcDurC 7 MF
     NcSalL

GHANA NEWS.
   Washington, D. C. 1962+
     NcSalL
     ScCOB (6)+

GHANA TODAY.
   (Ghana Ministry of External Affairs) Accra, Ghana.
   v1, 1957
     GAU (1-7)
     NcSalL
     ScCOB (12)+
     TNF (107)
     VHaI (1)-(3-6), (8-10)

GHANIAN.
   Accra, Ghana. no1, 1958-1966//
     GAU (1)
     VHaI (1)

GOLD COAST STORY.
      TNF

GOLDSBORO CHRISTIAN INSTITUTE.
    Goldsboro-Raleigh, North Carolina.
      TNDC

GUIDE.
      GAU O 6, 1898-Ag 1903 MF

GUIDE TO NEGRO PERIODICAL LITERATURE.
    Winston-Salem, North Carolina.  1 F 1941-S 1946//
      VHaI 2-4
      VUnU 1-2, 4

HAITI SUN.
      w
      TNF (J 9, 1953-D 5, 1954)

HALF CENTURY MAGAZINE.
    Chicago.  v1-18, Ag 1916-Ja/F 1925.
      AAM
      GA 2-18 MF
      TNF
      VUnV 1-18

HAMPTON ALUMNI JOURNAL.
    Hampton, Virginia.  v1-7, no1 Je 1924-1930
      ATT
      VHaI 1-7

HAMPTON ALUMNI RECORD.
    Hampton, Virginia.  v1-12, Ja 1959-1969//
      VHaI 1-12

HAMPTON ANNUAL.
    Hampton, Virginia.  v1, 1962+
      VHaI

HAMPTON BULLETIN.
    Hampton, Virginia. (Supersedes: Hampton Alumni
    Journal and Hampton Alumni Record)
       NcRR
       TNF (43)
       VHaI (9-55)

HAMPTON INSTITUTE LETTER.
    Hampton, Virginia.
       VHaI 6

HAMPTON LEAFLETS.
    Hampton Virginia. 1905-1921// (Absorbed Hampton
    Agriculture Leaflet, Hampton Animal-Industry Leaflet
    and Hampton Nature-Study Leaflet)
       TNF
       VHaI

HAMPTON NEGRO CONFERENCE ANNUAL REPORT.
    Hampton, Virginia. 1-16, 1897-1912// (1 in Southern
    Workman)
       ATT 2-16
       VHaI 1-16

HAMPTON SCRIPT.
    Hampton, Virginia. v1, 1928+
       VHaI 1+

HAMPTON STUDENT.
    Hampton, Virginia. v1-16, 1909-1927//
       ATT (1-16)
       VHaI 1-16

HARBARI.
       NcElcU

HARIJAN.
    Madras, India. 1933-56
       ATT 13

HARLEM QUARTERLY.
    New York. v1, 1949-1950//

(HARLEM QUARTERLY.)
      GA 1 MF
      ScU 1
      TNF (1)
      VHaI 1
      VUnV 1

HARVARD JOURNAL OF AFRO-AMERICAN AFFAIRS.
    Cambridge, Massachusetts.  v2, no2, 1971+  (Formerly:
    Harvard Journal of Negro Affairs)
      NcElcU
      NcFayS 2
      VCwM (2)
      VHaI (2)
      VNsC (2)
      VUnU (2)
      VUnV (2)

HARVARD JOURNAL OF NEGRO AFFAIRS.
    Cambridge, Massachusetts.  v1-2, no1, 1965-1968.
    See also Harvard Journal of Afro-American Affairs
      ATT 1
      ScRHW 2+

HAWKS CRY.
    Tuskegee, Alabama.
      ATT 3-4

HEAD START.
    Newsletter.  Washington, D. C.  1966+
      TJoS

HEADLINES AND PICTURES; A MONTHLY NEGRO NEWS REVIEW.
    Detroit, Michigan.  v1-3, no3, Jl 1944-S 1946//
      TNF 2
      VUnV 2

HEEBIES JEEBIES.
    Chicago.  1924.
      ATT 1

HELPER MAGAZINE.
    Harvey, Illinois.  vl, 1898?+
        GAU 1

HELPING HAND.
        A-AR D 13, 1912-D 1, 1916

HERALD.
        A-AR S 25, 1886-Ag 6, 1887
        TNF

HERALD-DISPATCH.
    (National edition) Los Angeles.  1952+
        TNF
        VHaI +
        VUnU +

HERALD OF FREEDOM.
    (New Hampshire Anti-Slavery Society) Concord, New
    Hampshire.  1-10 (nol-480), Mr 7, 1835-Mr 7, 1845;
    ns vl-2, no4, Mr 14, 1845-O 23, 1846//
        ATT 7-9

HERALD OF HOLINESS.
    Kansas City, Missouri.  1, Ap 17, 1912+
        TNF (O 29, 1945-Je 10, 1946)

HOME CIRCUIT.
        TNF

HOME MISSION COLLEGE REVIEW.
    (American Baptist Home Mission Society of New York)
    Philadelphia.  vl-4, nol, My 1927-My 1930//
        TNF 1-2, (3-4)
        VUnV (1-2)-(4)

HOME STUDY COURSE.
    Nashville.
        TNBPB

HOPE; ORGAN OF THE FIRESIDE SCHOOLS.
    Nashville.  1, S 1885+
        TNF (Mr 1940-My 1961)

HORIZON; A JOURNAL OF THE COLOR LINE.
    Alexandria, Virginia.  1-4, 1907-1908//
        ATT 1-4
        GAU 1-3
        TNF (1-4)
        VHaI (1-6)

HOWARD LAW JOURNAL.
    (Howard University School of Law) Washington, D. C.
    v1, 1955+
        ScCOB (13-14)+
        VHaI (6-7), (11-13), (16)
        VNsC 11+

HOWARD REVIEW.
    (Howard University) Washington, D. C.  v1-2, Je 1923-
    Ja 1925//
        TNF 1
        VUnV (1-2)

HOWARD UNIVERSITY BULLETIN AND RECORD MAGAZINE.
        ATT

HOWARD UNIVERSITY MAGAZINE.
        NcRR

HOWARD UNIVERSITY RECORD.
    (Howard University) Washington, D. C.  v1-19, no8,
    1907-Je 1925//
        TNF (16-17)

HOWARD'S AMERICAN MAGAZINE; DEVOTED TO THE COLORED RACE.
    Harrisburg, Pennsylvania.  1-6, 1890-Ap 1901//  (1-
    Howard's Negro American Monthly)
        GAU (6)
        VHaI (4), (6)

HUE.
    Chicago.  vl, 1954+
        TNF

HUNT'S MAGAZINE AND COMMERCIAL REVIEW.
        TNF

HUNTSVILLE GAZETTE.
    w Huntsville, Alabama.  N 22, 1879-D 29, 1894//
        AAM
        A-AR (My 28, 1881-Mr 10, 1883)
        VStC

HUNTSVILLE JOURNAL.
    w Huntsville, Alabama.  Ja 5, 1895-1912//?
        A-AR (Ag 4, 1899-D 1905), J 1906-F 1912

HUNTSVILLE STAR.
    w Huntsville, Alabama.  Ja 26, 1900+
        AAM

IRCD BULLETIN.
    (Information Retrieval Center On the Disadvantaged)
    New York.  1, Ja 1965+
        NcWU 6+

IMANI MAGAZINE.
    (Communications Workshop of the Black Allied Student
    Association of New York University) New York.
    F 1971+
        ATT 5
        NcElcU

IMPERIAL NIGHTHAWK.
    (Knights of the Ku Klux Klan) Atlanta, Georgia.
    Mr 28, 1923-N 19, 1924//
        ATT Mr 28, 1923-N 14, 1924
        GAU Mr 28, 1923-N 14, 1924
        VHaI 1923-1924 MF
        VUnU 1923-1923 MF

INDEPENDENT.
> New York.  vl-121, no89 (nol-4089) D 7, 1848-0 13,
> 1928//
>> ATT 69
>> GAU (52-53), (56-106), 107, (110-111), 112,
>> (114-121)
>> ScGRVF 50-105, 107-121
>> ScSpW 65-102
>> TNF (58)
>> VUnV

INDEX TO PERIODICAL ARTICLES BY AND ABOUT NEGROES.
> Wilberforce, Ohio.  vl, 1950+  (Formerly:  Index to
> Selected Periodicals)
>> AAM 18
>> GA 1-19
>> NcCoB 1-20
>> NcDaD 1
>> NcElcU 1
>> NcRR 10
>> VCwM 16+
>> VFsR 16+
>> VHaI 16+
>> VRpL 16-20
>> VUnU 16+
>> VUnV 16+

INDEX TO SELECTED PERIODICALS.
> Decennial cumulation 1950-59, vl-10, -15//  (Title
> change to Index to Periodical Articles by and About
> Negroes.  vl6+)  See also Index to Periodical
> Articles By and About Negroes
>> ScOrS 1-15, 16-18, 19-20
>> TNF
>> VCwM 1-15
>> VFsR 1-15
>> VHaI 1-15
>> VRpL 11-15
>> VUnU 1-15
>> VUnV 1-15

INDUSTRIAL STATESMAN.
   Philadelphia. v1, 1960+
      GAU

INFO.
   Gary, Indiana. w 1, Ja 1953+
      VHaI

INFORMER.
   w Houston, Texas. My 24, 1919+ (Ja 10, 1931-Jl, 28,
   1934 as Houston Informer and Texas Freeman)
      GAU 1962-1964
      NcD 1972+

INLAND AFRICA.
   (Africa Inland Mission) New York. 1, 1917+
      TNJ-S (49-54)

INSTITUT D'ETUDES CENTRAFRICAINES.
   Brazzaville, Congo. 1945
      ATT 1

INSTITUT DE FRANCAIS.
   Bulletin
      ATT 17-19
      TNF 17, 18, 20-21

INSTITUT FRANCAIS D'AFRIQUE NOIRE.
   Paris. Bulletin. 1 Ja 1939+
      TNF (17), 18, 20-21

INTEGRATED EDUCATION RACE AND SCHOOLS.
   Chicago. 1, 1963+
      AAM 9
      ATT 1+
      NcDurC 1+
      NcElcU 1+
      NcFayS 7+
      NcGU 1+
      NcRS 7+
      ScCOB
      ScOrC 7+

(INTEGRATED EDUCATION RACE AND SCHOOLS.)
  TJoS
  TNF 1-2, (3-4)
  TNLO
  TNMe 1+
  VHaI 3+
  VNsC 7+
  VStC


INTERCOM.
  New York. 1959+
   GA 12


INTERCULTURAL NEWS.
  TNF


INTERMEDIATE EDITION OF VACATION CHURCH SCHOOL.
  Nashville.
   TNBPB


INTERMEDIATE QUARTERLY.
  Nashville. 1881-1922//
   TNBPB


INTERNATIONAL CONFERENCE OF NEGRO WORKERS.
  Proceedings and Decisions
   ATT


INTERNATIONAL QUARTERLY.
  Burlington, Vermont; New York. 1-12, 1900-1906//
   TNF (5)


INTERRACIAL BOOKS FOR CHILDREN.
  New York. 1967+
   NcElcU


INTERRACIAL NEWSLETTER.
  (Friends General Conference) Pittman, New Jersey.
  v1, 1927-?
   VUnV (1-2), (6-8)-10, (12)

INTERRACIAL NEWS SERVICE.
   (Federal Council of the Churches of Christ in
   America.  Race Relations Department) New York.  1,
   1930+  (Numbering begins with 9, 1938)
      VHaI 10-24
      VUnV (5), (8), 11, 17
      VUtS (1-5)-(13)-36

INTERRACIAL REVIEW.
   (Federated Colored Catholics of the U.S.) St. Louis,
   Missouri.  1, 1928+  (v1-2, no9, 1928-S 1929 as
   St. Elizabeth's Chronicle; v2, no10-v5, no9, O 1929-
   S 1932 Chronicle)
      ATT 1-39
      GAU (1-39)
      NcDurC 36+
      NcRR 35-(39)
      TNF 7-17, (20), 21-24, (25), 26-29, (30), 31-37
      VHaI (8-9)-(11)-(13-18)-(20-22)-(27)-(29) (33)-
      39MF
      VUnU MF
      VUnV (15)

INVENTORY OF RESEARCH IN RACIAL AND CULTURAL RELATIONS.
   Chicago.  v1, 1948
      ATT 1-5
      TNF 2-3, (4)
      VHaI (1), (3)
      VUnV 1-5

IOTA KAPPA LAMBDA JOURNAL.
   New York.  v1, 1933?+
      TNF

IOWA STATE BYSTANDERS.
   Des Moines, Iowa.  1894+
      VsTC

IVY LEAF.
   (Official Organ of the Alpha Kappa Sorority)
   Chicago.  v28, 1922+

(IVY LEAF.)
        ATT 7
        TNF (24-25), (31-34)
        VHaI (28), (30-31), (43-44), (46)

JACKSON (MISSISSIPPI) ADVOCATE.
        ATT
        TNMe My 27, 1961-D 1968 MF

JAMAICA CHRISTIAN.
        TNDC

JAMAICA CHRISTIAN MISSION.
        TNDC

JAMAICA CHRISTIAN PIONEER.
        TNDC

JAMAICA DISCIPLE.
        TNDC

JAMAICA FIELD NEWS.
     (United Christian Missionary Society) Indianapolis.
        TNDC

JAMAICA NEWSLETTER.
     (USMS; Phillips Family)
        TNDC

JAMAICA WEEKLY GLEANER.
     Kingston, Jamaica, British West Indies.
        ATT
        VHaI (1952-53)
        VHoC (1971)+

JAMAICAN HISTORICAL REVIEW.
     Kingston, British West Indies.  vl, Je 1945+
        VCwM 1+

JANA; THE NEWS MAGAZINE OF RESURGENT ASIA AND AFRICA.
     Colombo, Ceylon.
        VUnV (3-4)

JARVIS GAZETTE.
    (Jarvis Christian College) Hawkins, Texas.
      TNDC

JARVISONIAN.
    (Jarvis Christian College) Hawkins, Texas.
      TNDC

JAZZ MUSIC.
    London. 1, 1942+
      TNF

JET.
    (Johnson Publishing Company, Inc.) Chicago. v1,
    1951+
      AAM 37
      ATT 34
      GA 36, 34-37 MF
      GAU (11)-12-(13-18), (20-26)
      NcCJ 6
      NcCO 30
      NcCoB +
      NcDur
      NcDurC 1
      NcEC
      NcElcU
      NcFayS 34
      NcFB
      NcHY
      NcL
      NcLK
      NcRR 29
      NcSalL 28
      ScCOB (23, 25-35)+
      ScOrC (15-18, 21-31, 33-36)
      ScOrS 19-21, MF, 16-41
      TK
      TKM
      TMVH
      TNF (1-34)
      TNK
      TN-H

(JET.)
        TNW
        TOR
        TRR
        VcoU 39+
        VCvC 39+
        VFeC 35+
        VFsR (41)+
        VHaI (3-10)-(12-27)-(29)-(31)-(33-34)-(36-37)
        VKpL (41)+
        VNsC 35+
        VSsH
        VStC
        VTnC 39-(40)
        VUnU (39)+
        VUnV 38+
        VUtS
        VVaC


JEUNE AFRIQUE.
    (Union Africaine des arts et des Lettres)
    Elizabethville, Belgian Congo.  n4, 1948+
        VCwM 457+


JOHN F. SLATER FUND OCCASIONAL PAPERS.
    Baltimore, Maryland.  1-29, 1894-1935//
        ATT 1-29
        TNF 6, 11


JOHN F. SLATER FUND PROCEEDINGS AND REPORTS.
    1882-1936/37
        ATT 1882-1936/37


JOURNAL AND GUIDE.
    Norfolk, Virginia.  1899+
        GAU 25-29 MF, 41-48, 49 MF (51-52) MF, 62, 65-66
        NcCJ
        NcCO
        NcD
        NcDurC 1
        NcEC

(JOURNAL AND GUIDE.)
    NcE1cU
    NcFayS 69+
    NcL
    NcRR 69+
    NcRSA
    NcRSH
    S.D. Bishop +
    TKM
    TNF
    TNJ-S
    TNK
    VCvC
    VDpL
    VHaI 18-19, 24+
    VKpL (18-19)+
    VMwC 18-19, 24-26, 66+
    VNnP
    VNsC
    VRoP 72+
    VRpL
    VStC
    VStL 18-19, 25+
    VUnU MF 16-17, 21+
    VVaC

JOURNAL OF AFRICAN ADMINISTRATION.
    (Great Britain Colonial Office.  African Studies
    Branch) London.  1-13 no4, 1949-0 1961
    TNF

JOURNAL OF AFRICAN-AMERICAN STUDIES.
    Annual.  (Hampton Institute) Hampton, Virginia.
    1972+
    VHaI 1+
    VUnV 1+

JOURNAL OF AFRICAN HISTORY.
    New York.  1960
    ATT 1+
    GA 1
    GAMB 1-2, 5-6
    GAU 1-9

(JOURNAL OF AFRICAN HISTORY.)
        NcBoA 1+
        NcCoB 9+
        NcDaD 1+
        NcElcU 1+
        NcFayS
        NcRR 1+
        NcRSH
        NcSalL 1-12 MF 1971+
        ScCLEA 8+
        ScCOB
        ScCoC 10+
        ScOrC 11+
        ScOrS 1-8, 9-12 MF
        TJeCN 1+
        TM-SW 1
        TMU 11+
        TNBK 9+
        TNF 1-(2)-10
        TNJ-S 1+
        TNMe 1+
        VCoU 12+
        VHaI (1)-(10)+
        VMaC 1+
        VNsC (1-7), 9+
        VUnV 1+

JOURNAL OF AFRICAN LANGUAGES.
    London.  v1-11, no2/3, 1962-73//
        NcDurC 1+
        TNF 1-6

JOURNAL OF AFRICAN SOCIETY.
    1901?
        TNF 1-20

JOURNAL OF AFRICAN STUDIES.
        VCoU

JOURNAL OF ASIAN AND AFRICAN STUDIES.
    Leiden, Netherlands.  v1, 1967+

(JOURNAL OF ASIAN AND AFRICAN STUDIES.)
      ScRHW 4+
      TNJ-S 1+
      VCwM 1+
      VUnV 1+

JOURNAL OF BLACK POETRY.
   San Francisco. 1966+
      ATT 1
      GA 4
      NcElcU
      NcFayS
      NcRSA
      TNF
      VCoU 6+
      VUnV 1+

JOURNAL OF BLACK STUDIES.
   (Sage Publications, Inc.) Beverly Hills, California.
   1970+
      GA 2
      NcCJ (2)
      NcCoB 3+
      NcElcU
      NcGU
      NcSalL 2
      ScCOB
      ScOrC 1+
      ScRHW 1+
      VCoU 2+
      VCwM 1+
      VFsR (2)+
      VHaI 2+
      VUnV 1+

JOURNAL OF BLACK STUDIES AND RESEARCH.
   1970+
      TJqS
      TM-SW 1
      TNF
      TNMe 1

JOURNAL OF ETHNIC STUDIES.
    TMaU

JOURNAL OF HUMAN RELATIONS.
    (Central State University) Wilberforce, Ohio.  vl,
    1951+
        GAU (1)-2-5-(6)-7-14
        NcDurC 11+
        NcElcU 18+
        NcGrE 1-10 MF
        NcRS 1+
        NcSalL 1+
        ScCoC 1-16+
        ScGRVF 15+
        ScOrC (4), 6-(13-14, 20)+
        TNF (1), (3)
        VHaI 10+
        VMaC (14)+
        VUnU 11+
        VUnV (2), (4), (14), (16)+

JOURNAL OF INTERGROUP RELATIONS.
    (National Association of Intergroup Relations
    Officials) New York.  vl, nol-6, My 1958-F 1960
        ATT 1-2
        GAU (1)-(4)
        NcDurC 1-4
        NcRS 1
        TNF (1)
        VUtS 1-(2)-5

JOURNAL OF THE INTERNATIONAL AFRICAN INSTITUTE.
    NcRR

JOURNAL OF LOCAL ADMINISTRATION OVERSEAS.
    London.  1962+  (Title changed to:  Journal of
    Administration Overseas)
        TNF 1-3

JOURNAL OF MODERN AFRICAN STUDIES.
    New York.  1963+

(JOURNAL OF MODERN AFRICAN STUDIES.)
        ATT 1
        NcBoA 1, 3, 5, 8
        NcElcU 8+
        NcFayS
        NcGuG
        NcRSA 10
        NcRSH
        ScCOB 6+
        ScGRVF 1+
        ScOrC 1
        ScRHW 1+
        TMaU 9, 10
        TNBK 7+
        TNF 1-7
        TNJ-S 1
        TNMe 1+
        VCwM 1+
        VHaI 9+
        VMaC 2+
        VRmW 6+
        VUnV 1+
        VUtS 1+


JOURNAL OF NEGRO EDUCATION.
    (Howard University.  College of Education, Washington)
    Lancaster, Pennsylvania.  1 Ap 1932+
        AAM 2-3, 10-12, 14-23, 26-27, 32, 36-37
        ATT 1+
        GA 1-34 MF
        GACC 9, (18), 19-21, (23-26)
        GAMB 10, (13), (18), (25), (28), 30, 32, 34, 36,
         38
        GAU (1), 2, (3-4), 5, (6-9), 10, (34-35), 38
        NcBE 26
        NcBoC 19+
        NcCJ 28, 37, 39, 41
        NcCuW 29, 36, 38+
        NcDaD 1-35, 36, 37+
        NcDurC
        NcElcU 1+
        NcFayS 1+
        NcFB 12-39

(JOURNAL OF NEGRO EDUCATION.)
       NcGU 1+
       NcRR 2+
       NcRS 1+
       NcSalL 14+
       NcWS
       S.D. Bishop 13+
       ScCLEA 1+
       ScCOB 1, (32), 36+
       ScCoC 1+
       ScGAL 38-
       ScGORC 6, (12), 15, 31, (33), 35, (37)
       ScGRVF 1+
       ScOrC 1+
       ScOrS 1-13, 15-28, 30, 32-36, 1-40 MF
       ScRHW 38+
       ScSpW 17+
       ScU 1+
       TJeCN 33+
       TJóS
       TMaU 40-41
       TMU 1+
       TNBK 30+
       TND
       TNF 1-22, (23-24), 25-39
       TNK
       TNJ
       TNJ-S 14, (22), 25+
       TNL 16, 19-20, 23-24, 28-29, 30-31, 33, 39
       TNLO
       TNMa 1-26 MF, 27+
       TNMe 32+
       TNMO 26, 30-35, 37, 38, 61-66, 68, 69
       TRR
       VCoU 40+
       VCwM 1+
       VGmC 40+
       VFsR 41+
       VHaI 1+
       VHoC (39)+
       VMaC 38+

(JOURNAL OF NEGRO EDUCATION.)
  VMwC 1-18, 25+
  VNnP
  VNsC 1-2, 4-5, 7-8, 10-12, 14-31, 36+
  VRaC 26+
  VRbC (39)-40
  VRmW 14+
  VRoP 39+
  VRpL 1+
  VStC
  VUnU 1+
  VUnV 1+

JOURNAL OF NEGRO HISTORY.
  (Association for the Study of Negro Life and
  History) Washington, D. C.  1, 1916+
   AAM 1-2, 4, 7-44, 47, 49, 51-53, 54+
   ATT 1+
   GA 1+
   GACC 1-53, 55
   GAMB 1-2, 4, 6-8, 10-15, 17, 19-24, 26-53
   GASC 1-53
   GAU 1-51
   NcBE 1-49 MF
   NcBoA 1+
   NcBuC 1-53
   NcCJ 1-7, 9-26
   NcCoB 16-21, 41-42, 46, 53, 56-57
   NcCQ
   NcCU 1-44 MF, 59+
   NcCuW 1+
   NcDaD 1-11, 15-17, 29-30, 33, 35, 39-41, 45+
   NcDur
   NcDurC 1+
   NcElcU 1+
   NcFayC
   NcFayS 10+
   NcFB
   NcGrS
   NcGU 1+
   NcGuG
   NcHYL 1+

(JOURNAL OF NEGRO HISTORY.)
     NcRR 1+
     NcRS 1+
     NcRSA
     NcRSH
     NcSalL 1-49 MF, 51+
     NcWS 1-2, 9-14, 31-35, 38, 40+
     NcWU 1
     S.D. Bishop 29+
     ScCLEA 1+
     ScCOB 1-43, 45-(53)+
     ScCoC 1-47, (48)-49+
     ScGal 54+
     ScGRVF 50+
     ScOrC 1-12, 34-40 MF
     ScOrS 1-49, 1-54, 56, 57 MF
     ScRHW 1-50, (51-52), 53-54
     ScU 1+
     TD 45+ MF
     TDB 1+
     TJeCN 1+
     TJoS
     TJL
     TK
     TKM
     TMNH
     TM-SW 47+
     TMU (1-44)-45+
     TNBK 42+
     TND
     TNF 1-(9)-10, 12-16, 18-(46)-(50)-55
     TN-H
     TNJ 56+
     TNJ-S 41-53, (54), 55+
     TNK
     TNL 28, 31-34, 37-39, 42-45, 48-49, 52
     TNLO
     TNMa 1-26 MF, 27+
     TNMe 1+
     TNMO 3-4, 6, 9-10, 13, 16-17, 24, 29, 31, 46, 48,
      49

(JOURNAL OF NEGRO HISTORY.)
      TPM
      TRR
      TTM
      VChT 45+ MF
      VClV
      VCnC 55+
      VCoU 25-27, 54, 56+
      VCpL (55)+
      VCvC 56+; MF 41-55
      VCwM 1+
      VFsR (56)+; MF 1-55
      VGmC 53+
      VHaI 1+
      VHcC 56+; MF 45-55
      VHoC (55-56)+
      VHsC 2, 4, 6, 41+
      VKpL 51+
      VMaC 1+; MF 1-48
      VMbC 53+
      VMcV 54+
      VMwC 1+
      VNnP
      VNsC 1-50, 52+
      VPhC 1+
      VRaC 1+
      VRbC 53-56
      VRcP 32+
      VRmC 1+
      VRmW 10+
      VRoP 1+
      VRpL 14-(36)-(52)+
      VStC
      VSuC 49+
      VTnC 43-56
      VUnR 1+
      VUnU 1-2, 4, 6, 16, 18, 23, 26, 29, 32, 40, 42,
       43; MF 44+
      VUnV 1+
      VUtS (1), 14-(16), (23), 29+

JOURNAL OF RACE DEVELOPMENT.
　　Worcester, Massachusetts.　v1-9, 1910-Je 1919.
　　(Supersedes:　Journal of International Relations.
　　v1-12, no4, Jl 1910-Ap 1922//)
　　　　ATT 4

JOURNAL OF RELIGION IN AFRICA.
　　Leiden, Netherlands.　1967+
　　　　TNJ-S 1+

JOURNAL OF RELIGIOUS EDUCATION.
　　Nashville.　1936+
　　　　TNF (7), 8, (9), 10, (11-12), 13-16, (17-20),
　　　　　21-22, (23-25), 26-27, (28-29), 30-33

JOURNAL OF RELIGIOUS THOUGHT.
　　(School of Religion, Howard University) Washington,
　　D. C.　v1, 1943
　　　　NcDurC 11+
　　　　NcSalL 18+
　　　　TNF 1, 3-(4), (6)-25
　　　　VHaI (1-3), (22-23)
　　　　VUtS 1+

JOURNAL OF WEST AFRICAN LANGUAGES.
　　New York.　1964+
　　　　VNsC 6+

JUBILEE.
　　　　TNF

JUNIOR PUPIL'S MANUAL OF VACATION CHURCH SCHOOL.
　　Nashville.
　　　　TNSPB

JUNIOR QUARTERLY.
　　Nashville.
　　　　TNBPB

JUNIOR SCHOOL LESSONS.
　　Nashville.
　　　　TNSPB

KNEA JOURNAL.
    (Kentucky Negro Education Association) Louisville,
    Kentucky.  vl, 1931+
        TNF

KYK OVER DELTA L.
        TNG

KANSAS CITY CALL.
    w Kansas City, Missouri.  My 1919+
        ATT 1968+
        NcCJ
        NcDurC N 1951+
        TNLO

KAPPA ALPHA PSI JOURNAL.
    Nashville.  1914+
        ATT 10
        GAU (26-29), (43), (46)-49
        TNF (20), (22-23), (27-28), (30-34), 39, (40-43),
        44, (45-50)-51-(52)-54

KINDERGARTEN BIBLE LESSONS.
    Nashville.
        TNSPB

KINDERGARTEN EDITION OF VACATION CHURCH SCHOOL.
    Nashville.
        TNSPB

LANCET.
    Petersburg, Virginia.
        VStC

LANGUAGE ASSOCIATION OF EASTERN AFRICA JOURNAL.
    Nairobi, Kenya.  vl, 1970+
        TNF

LEAGUE OF COLOURED PEOPLES NEWSLETTER.
    London.  1, 1940+
        ATT 17

LIBERATION.
    New York.  v1, 1956
        ATT 14
        NcDurC 7+
        NcRS 13+
        TNF 6-7
        VHaI 9-12
        VUnV (1)-(10-11)-13-14
        VUtS (5), (10)

LIBERATOR.
    Boston.  1-35, Ja 1, 1831-D 29, 1865//
        ATT 1-35 MF
        GAMB 1-35
        GAU 1-35 MF
        NcDurC 1-35 MF
        ScCOB
        ScU 1-35 MF
        TNF
        TNMe 1-35 MF
        TRR
        VHaI 2-35 MF
        VUnU 1-35 MF
        VUnV (1)

LIBERATOR.
    (American Negro Labor Congress) Chicago.  v1-3, no46,
    1925-D 15, 1932 (no1-33, 1925-My 25, 1929 as Negro
    Champion.  Superseded by Harlem Liberator, later
    Negro Liberator)
        ATT 1-3 MF
        GAMB (1)
        GAU 1-3 MF

LIBERATOR.
    (Afro-American Research Institute, Inc.) New York.
    v1, 1960+
        VCoU 11+
        VCwM 10+
        VFrB 2+
        VFsR 11+
        VHaI (9)+

LIBERIA.
    Monrovia, Liberia.  vl, 1922+
        NcRR

LIBERIA.
    (American Colonization Society) Washington, D. C.
    nol-34, N 1892-F 1909//  (Supersedes:  African
    Repository)
        ATT 26-34
        ScU 1-34

LIBERIA AND WEST AFRICA.
    Monrovia, Liberia.  1-21, 1899-1920//?
        VHaI (7-8)

LIBERIA TODAY.
    Washington, D. C.  vl, 1952
        ATT 1-4
        TNF 1-4-(5-7)
        VHaI (1)-(4-9)

LIBERIAN STUDIES JOURNAL.
    Newark, Delaware.  vl, 1968+
        VCwM 1+

LIBERTY TREE; A MONTHLY PUBLICATION DEVOTED TO THE ANTI-
SLAVERY CAUSE.
    Chicago.  1-3, 1843-O 1846//
        TNF 2

LIBRARY SERVICE REVIEW.
    (North Carolina Negro Library Association) Durham,
    North Carolina.  vl-2, nol, 1953-O 1955//
        NcRR

LIGHT OF THE WORLD.
    vl, 1920
        ATT 2

LITERARY JOURNAL.
        TNF

LIVING AGE.
 Boston. 1, 1844-1941//
  ScDWE 327-(329-330)-(332)-345
  ScGRVF 1-2, 6, 15-26, 28-35, 37-70, 72-91, 93-145,
   147-153, 155, 157-158, 160-161, 165, 170-171,
   178, 188, 312-338, 356-360
  ScSPC 357-360
  ScSpW 28-344

LIVING BLUES.
 Chicago. 1970+
  GA 2+

LIVINGSTONIA NEWS.
 Livingstonia, Northern Rhodesia. 1-10, 1908-1919//
 (v11 pub. 1924) (Supersedes: Aurora; a journal of
 missionary news and Christian work)
  VHaI (2), (4-6), (9-11)

LONDON UNIVERSITY. SCHOOL OF ORIENTAL AND AFRICAN
STUDIES BULLETIN.
 1, 1971+
  ScRHW 28+

LOS ANGELES EAGLE.
 w Mr 8, 1879+
  GAU 1-37

LOS ANGELES SENTINEL.
 w My 18, 1933+
  GAU F-Mr 1945, S 1946, 1954

LOUISIANA COLORED TEACHER'S JOURNAL.
 Baton Rouge, Louisiana. 1, 1925+
  VHaI (11)

LOUISIANA WEEKLY.
 New Orleans, Louisiana. 1925+
  GAU 1937, 1958-59, 1961-64

LOUISIANIAN.
 New Orleans, Louisiana.
  VStC

LOUISVILLE DEFENDER.
   Louisville, Kentucky.
     TNF
     TNMe 1951-1969

LOUISVILLE LEADER.
   Louisville, Kentucky.
     GAU

MCGIRT'S MAGAZINE.
   Philadelphia, Pennsylvania.  vl, nol, 2, 4, Jn-
   Mr, S, O-D, 1909//
     GAU 1

MAKERERE JOURNAL.
   Kampala, Uganda.  vl, 1958+
     ATT 2
     TNF

MANHATTAN TRIBUNE.
     TNF
     TRR

MASONIC JOURNAL.
     NcElcU

MASSACHUSETTS ANTI-SLAVERY SOCIETY.
   (1833-35 as New England Anti-Slavery Society)
   (Superseded by American Anti-Slavery Society)
   Annual Report.  Boston.  1-21, 1833-53//
     ATT 2-8

MASTER MUSICIAN.
   Philadelphia.  vl, nol-8, 1919-Ag 1920//  (Supersedes: American Musician and Sportsman Magazine)
   v2, no9, 1920-22//
     ATT 1

MEHARRY MEDICAL COLLEGE QUARTERLY DIGEST.
   Nashville.  vl, 1962?+
     AAM
     TNF

MEMPHIS WORLD.
  TNLO
  TNMe Jl 26, 1931+ MF

MESSAGE.
  (Association of Baptists for Evangelism in the Orient)
  Marblehead, Massachusetts. 1, 1935+
    TNF (2-6), (9), 10-11, (12), 13-14, (15), 16-24,
    (25-33)
    VHaI (20), (28-30), (32-33)

MESSAGE MAGAZINE.
  Nashville. 1, 1935+
    NcCJ (37-38)
    NcRR 12-13, 36+
    NcSalL

MESSENGER.
  Hagerstown, Maryland.
    TNDC

MESSENGER: WORLD'S GREATEST NEGRO MONTHLY.
  New York. v1-10, no5, 1917 My/Je 1928//
    AAM 1-10
    ATT 1-10 MF
    GA 1-10 MF
    GAMB (1)-10
    GAU 1-10
    TNF 1-10
    TN-H
    TNMe 1-10
    VHaI 1-10 MF
    VStC
    VUnU 1-10 MF
    VUnV (2), 9-10

MESSENGER MONTHLY ADVERTISER.
  TNF

METROPOLITAN.
  Glenview, Illinois. 1904+
    ScDWE 63+

MICHIGAN CHRONICLE.
    Detroit, Michigan.  1936+
        GAU 1961-64
        NcSalL
        TNF
        VHaI +

MIDWEST JOURNAL.
    Jefferson City, Missouri.  1, Winter, 1948 Sp/Fall
    56//  (Supersedes the University's Research Bulletin,
    v1-8//)
        GAU (5)
        TNF (1-2), (5), 6-7, (8)
        VHaI (1)-(7-8)
        VUnV (1)

MILITANT.
    New York.  v1, 1936?+
        VNsC

MIRROR.
        ScSpW 2-4

MISSION HERALD.
    (Foreign Mission Board:  National Baptist Convention)
    Louisville, Kentucky.  1, 1897+
        TNF (47), 56

MISSION NEWS.
    (Disciples of Christ Congo Mission)
        TNDC

MISSIONARY HERALD.
    (Baptist Missionary Society) London.  1, 1919+
        TNF 2-28, 30-35, 52, 62, 71, 74-75, 80-81

MISSIONARY HERALD AT HOME AND ABROAD.
    (American Board of Commissioners for Foreign
    Missions) Boston.   1 Jl 1805+
        TNF (139-141), (145-146)

MISSIONARY SEER.
   (African Methodist Episcopal Zion Church in America.
   Domestic and Foreign Missions) Washington, D. C.  1,
   1900+
      NcSalL
      TNF
      VHaI (51-54), (60-61)-(63)-(66)-(69)

MISSIONARY SUN.
      TNF

MISSISSIPPI EDUCATIONAL JOURNAL.
   (Mississippi Association of Teachers in Colored
   Schools) Jackson, Mississippi.  1, 1923+
      VHaI (13-15)

MISSISSIPPI FREE PRESS.
   w?  1961+
      GAU D22, 1962

MISSOURI ARGUS.
      TNMe My 22, 1835-N 22, 1839 MF

MOBILE BEACON.
      S.D. Bishop

MOBILE WEEKLY ADVOCATE.
      A-AR S 23, 1939-S 28, 1958

MOBILE WEEKLY PRESS.
   Mobile, Alabama.  1894+
      A-AR J 10, 1914-Ja 19, 1929

MODERN FARMER.
   (National Federation of Colored Farmers) Nashville.
   1, 1929+
      ATT 7

MONTHLY BULLETIN OF AFRICAN MATERIALS.
   (African Studies Center, Development Program)
   Brookline, Massachusetts.  1968+
      TNJ-S (1-2) 3+
      VHaI (3)+

*Newspapers and Periodicals by and about Black People*

MOON ILLUSTRATED WEEKLY.
    Memphis, Tennessee.  v1, 1906–1907//
        ATT 1
        GAU (1)
        TNF (1)
        VHaI (1)

MOREHOUSE COLLEGE BULLETIN.
    Atlanta, Georgia.  v1, 1932+
        AAM (38)
        GAU (1-2), (5-11), (17-19), (24-25), (27-31), (35)
        VHaI (32-35), (38)

MOREHOUSE JOURNAL OF SCIENCE.
    (Morehouse College) Atlanta, Georgia.  v1-5, no2,
    Ap 1926–Ap 1931//?
        ATT 3-5
        GAU (1-2), 3, (4-5), (15), (19)
        TNF (1), (3-6)-(15-16), (19)

MUHAMMED SPEAKS.
    Chicago.  1960+
        ATT (5) MF
        GAU (1-6)
        NcD 13+
        NcElcU
        NcRR 3-8, 12
        NcSalL
        TNF
        TRR
        VCoU 12
        VHaI 7, 9+ 5-6 MF
        VNsC +
        VUnU 5-6 MF

MUNGER AFRICANA LIBRARY NOTES.
    (California Institute of Technology) Pasadena,
    California.  v1, F 1971+
        TNJ-S (1)+

MUSIC AND POETRY.
    Chicago.   vl, nol-6, Ja-Je 1921//?
        ATT 1

MUTUAL BULLETIN.
    Durham, North Carolina.
        ATT

NATIONAL ALLIANCE.
    Washington, D. C.   1, 1915+
        NcCJ (54), (55)
        NcElcU
        VHaI (15-19)

NATIONAL ANTI-SLAVERY STANDARD.
    New York.   1-30, 1840-Ap 16, 1870; ns vl-3, My-
    Jl 1870; ns (3), vl-3, Jl 1870-D 1872// (Changed
    to:  National Standard)
        ATT (1-30), ns3 (1-2) MF
        GA 1-30 MF
        GAMB 1-3, ns3, 1-2
        GAU 1-30
        NcDurC 1-30, ns(3) 2 MF
        VHaI 1-30, ns3-ns(3) 2
        VUnU 1-30, ns3-ns(3) 2

NATIONAL ASSOCIATION FOR THE ADVANCEMENT OF COLORED
PEOPLE BULLETIN.
    New York.   1 D 1940+
        VHaI (5-8)

NATIONAL ASSOCIATION FOR THE ADVANCEMENT OF COLORED
PEOPLE REPORT.
    New York.   1, 1910+
        ATT 3+

NATIONAL ASSOCIATION OF COLLEGE WOMEN JOURNAL.
    Washington, D. C.
        TNF

NATIONAL ASSOCIATION OF COLLEGIATE DEANS AND REGISTRARS
IN NEGRO SCHOOLS PROCEEDINGS.
   Nashville.  1, 1926+
      ATT 6-11
      TNF (17-19)

NATIONAL ASSOCIATION OF NEGRO MUSICIANS MINUTES.
   Chicago.
      ATT

NATIONAL ASSOCIATION OF TEACHERS IN COLORED SCHOOLS.
   Bulletin.  vl-16, no1, 1922-F 1938//
      ATT 3+
      GAU (6), (8-9)
      VHaI (1, 6-15)

NATIONAL BAPTIST MAGAZINE.
   Nashville.  vl-7, no8, 1894-D 1900//?
      GAU (3)

NATIONAL BAPTIST UNION REVIEW.
   Nashville.  1, 1899+  (Early years as:  National
   Baptist Union)
      TNF

NATIONAL BAPTIST VOICE.
   Nashville.  1, 1915+
      TNF
      TNSPB 2+

NATIONAL BAR JOURNAL.
   (National Bar Association) St. Louis, Missouri.  1,
   Jl 1941+  (Suspended N 1941-My 1944)
      TNF (5-7)
      VHaI (2), (6)
      VUnV (1)

NATIONAL CONVENTION VOICE.
   St. Louis, Missouri.
      TNDC

NATIONAL EDUCATIONAL OUTLOOK AMONG NEGROES.
      Baltimore, Maryland.  vl-3, no5, 1937 My/Je 1940//
            ATT 1-3
            NcRR 1
            TNF 1-(3)
            VHaI 1-(3)
            VUnV 1-3


NATIONAL ERA.
      Washington, D. C.  1-14, 1847-1860//
            AAM 1-14 MF
            GA 1-14
            ScU 1-14 MF
            TMU 1-14
            VUnV 1-14 MF


NATIONAL EVANGELIST.
      Louisville, Kentucky.
            TNDC


NATIONAL FREEDMAN.
      (National Freedmen's Relief Association; American
      Freedman's Union Commission) New York.  vl-2, no9,
      1865-S 15, 1866//
            TNF (1-2)


NATIONAL MEDICAL ASSOCIATION JOURNAL.
      Tuskegee, Alabama.  1, 1909+
            ATT 1+
            GAU (1-2), (4), (7), 10, (12-14)-15, 17-31, (32)-
            33-(34)-35-(36)-37-(38-39)-41-(42)-46, (49)-57
            NcElcU 60+
            TNF (37), (40)
            VHaI 2, 4-5, 7-14, (18)-(23-24)-33-40)-(51)-
            (53-54)+
            VUvS


NATIONAL NEGRO BUSINESS LEAGUE PROCEEDINGS.
      Tuskegee, Alabama.  1-25, 1900-24//?
      (no23-24, 1922-23 never published)
            ATT 1-22, 25

NATIONAL NEGRO DENTAL ASSOCIATION BULLETIN.
Manassas, Virginia.  1, 1941+
VHaI (5-6)-11

NATIONAL NEGRO DIGEST.
Chicago.  v1, 1936?+
TNF (31-34)

NATIONAL NEGRO HEALTH NEWS.
(U.S. Public Health Service) Washington, D. C.
v1-18, no2, Ja/Mr 1933-Ap/Je 1950//   (Jl/S 1933,
Jl/S 1934 not published)
ATT 5-7
GA 1-18 MF
TNF (1-3), 4-(18)
VHaI (1), (4-9), (11-12), (15), 17-(18)
VNsC (1-18)
VUnV 1-18

NATIONAL NEGRO MIND.
TNF

NATIONAL NEGRO PRESS ASSOCIATION PROCEEDINGS.
ATT

NATIONAL NEGRO SCHOOL NEWS.
Tuskegee Institute, Alabama.  v3, 1912
ATT 1-4
VHaI (3)

NATIONAL NEGRO VOICE.
Kingston, Jamaica.  v1, no1-11, Jl 19-S 27, 1941//
(Running Title:  Negro Voice)
GA 1 MF
GAU
VHaI 1
VNsC 1
VUnV 1

NATIONAL NOTEBOOK QUARTERLY.
   (National Association of Teachers in Colored
   Schools) Augusta, Georgia.  1-3, 1918-21//?
      ATT 1-3
      VHaI (1-3)

NATIONAL NOTES.
   (National Association of Colored Women) Kansas City,
   Missouri.  1, 1899+  (Title varies:  National
   Association Notes)
      ATT 5-60

NATIONAL REPUBLICAN.
   d Washington, D. C.  N 26, 1860-Je 11, 1888//
      ScU Ja 1-Je 30, 1885 MF

NATIONAL TECHNICAL ASSOCIATION.
   Washington, D. C.  v1, 1950
      VHaI (3-8), (33), (36-38)

NATIONAL URBAN LEAGUE ANNUAL REPORT.
   New York.  1910+
      ATT 1+

NATIVE TEACHER'S JOURNAL.
   Pietermaritzburg, South Africa.  1, O 1919+
      VHaI (28), (30), (32-33)

NEGRO:  THE JOURNAL OF FACTS, PUBLISHED QUARTERLY BY THE
MIDWEST MUTUAL PUBLISHING HOUSE.
   St. Louis, Missouri.  v1 winter, 1943-44.  (My/Je
   1944 as:  Race)
      TNF
      VHaI (1-4)

NEGRO ACHIEVEMENTS.
   Fort Wayne, Indiana.  1952+
      TNF

NEGRO AMERICAN LITERATURE FORUM.
   Terre Haute, Indiana.  v1, 1967+

(NEGRO AMERICAN LITERATURE FORUM.)
  GA 1-4 MF, 5+
  NcSalL 5+
  ScCOB
  TNJ-S (1-3)
  VCoU 5+
  VCwM 1+
  VUnV (1), (5)

NEGRO AMERICAN MAGAZINE.
 San Antonio, Texas.  1922+
  ATT 4-7
  TNF (4), (8-9)

NEGRO BOOK CLUB NEWS.
 New York.  v1, 1946+
  TNF

NEGRO BRAILLE MAGAZINE.
 Louisville, Kentucky.  1952+
  NcDur

NEGRO BUSINESS.
 1939
  ATT 1
  GAU (1)
  TNF (1)

NEGRO BUSINESS AND FINANCIAL JOURNAL.
  TRR

NEGRO BUSINESS LEAGUE HERALD.
 (National Negro Business League) Tuskegee, Alabama.
 v1, 1912-?
  ATT 1

NEGRO COLLEGE QUARTERLY.
 Wilberforce, Ohio.  v1-5, no2, Mr 1943-Je 1947//
 See also Wilberforce University Quarterly
  ATT 2-5
  NcDurC 1-5
  NcElcU

(NEGRO COLLEGE QUARTERLY.)
        NcRR 1-4
        NcRSA
        TNF 1-(5)
        VHaI 1-(3)-(5)
        VStC
        VUnV 1-5


NEGRO DIGEST.
    Chicago.  1, N 1942-v19, My 1970//  (Title changed
    to:  Black World)  See also Black World
        ATT 1+
        GAU 1-(6)-7-(10-11)-16
        NcCJ (16-18)
        NcCO 17+
        NcCU 18+
        NcCuW 2-9
        NcDaD
        NcFayS 1-9, 18-19
        NcGU
        NcRR 11+
        ScCLEA 19+
        ScCOB (14), 18+
        ScOrC (1-9, 22-17)
        ScOrS 18
        ScRHW 22+
        ScU (1)
        TJoS
        TMMU
        TNF 1-(8-10), 11, (12-18)
        TNJ-S 2-3
        TNL 6-8, 14, 16
        VHaI (1)-19
        VMbC 18-19
        VNsC (3), (5), (7), (9), 18-19
        VRpL (18-19)
        VSrL
        VUnU (1)-(3), (5-8), (18)
        VuNV 1-(8), 9, (11)
        VUtS 4-10

NEGRO EDUCATIONAL REVIEW.
   (Florida Memorial College) St. Augustine, Florida.
   1950+
      AAM 10-11
      ATT 1-15
      GAU 1, 4, (5)-6, 10
      NcBoA 20+
      NcCU (16-19), 20
      NcElcU 1
      NcDurC 1
      NcFayS 6-15, 22
      NcGU 21+
      NcRSA
      NcSalL (1)+
      NcWS 4-12
      S.D. Bishop +
      ScCLEA 21+
      ScOrS 1, 3-4, 6-7
      TJoS
      TMU 21+
      TNF 1-(2)-15, (17), 19-20
      TNK
      TNL 1-2, 14
      TNMe 21+
      VHaI 1-(8)+
      VNsC (10-22)
      Voorhees
      VStC
      VUnU 1-3, 6, 13, 14

NEGRO FARMER.
   Tuskegee, Alabama.  1, Ap 1940+
      ATT 1-27

NEGRO FARMER AND MESSENGER.
   (Tuskegee Institute) Tuskegee, Alabama.  v1-5, no1,
   Ja 31, 1914-Ja 1918//
      ATT 1-5

NEGRO HERITAGE.
   Reston, Virginia.  1961+

(NEGRO HERITAGE.)
      ATT 1+
      NcBoA 1+
      NcBoC 9
      NcCoB 10+
      NcCU (5-8), 9+
      NcDurC 9+
      NcElcU 1+
      NcGU
      NcRR 1-8
      NcRSA
      NcSalL 1+
      ScCorC
      ScOrC 10
      VFsR (10)+
      VHaI 12+
      VNsC
      VStC
      VUnU (1-8), 11+

NEGRO HISTORICAL REVIEW.
      TOR

NEGRO HISTORY BULLETIN.
   (Association for the Study of Negro Life and History)
   Washington, D. C. 1, 0 1937+
      AAM 1-20, 26-27, 30-34
      ATT 1+
      AU (17), 18-30, 33
      GA 1-32, 33 MF, 35+
      GACC 11
      GAMB 1, 3-7, 9-16, 19-23, 28, 30-31
      GAU 1-(13)-14-(27-29)
      Nc
      NcALB
      NcAsbC 30+
      NcBE 17, 19
      NcBoA 9
      NcCJ (34), (35)
      NcCO 30+
      NcCoB 24-33 MF

(NEGRO HISTORY BULLETIN.)
        NcCU 31+
        NcCuW 33+
        NcDur
        NcDurC 8+
        NcElcU 1+
        NcFayC 15+
        NcFayS 1+
        NcFB
        NcGrE
        NcHP
        NcLK
        NcRR 4+
        NcRS 1+
        NcRSA
        NcRSH
        NcSalC 36+
        NcSalL 1-27, 33+
        NcWS 22-28
        NcY 35+
        S.D. Bishop 1, 3-19, 21+
        ScCLEA 34+
        ScCOB (12-13, 20-31)+
        ScOrC (1-9, 12-17), MF 18-19, 27-31+
        ScOrS 28, MF 17-29, 30-31, 34
        TJeCN 35+
        TJoS
        TK
        TMaU 17-35
        TMU
        TNF 1-12, 14-(27-29), 30-31
        TNJ 33+
        TNJ-S (18-19)20, (21), 22-24, (25), 26, 28-30,
         (31), 32+
        TNLO
        TNMA 27, 32+
        TNMe 1+
        TTM
        VChT 24+ MF
        VCnC 34+
        VCpL (25)+
        VCrR 32+

(NEGRO HISTORY BULLETIN.)
    VCvC 34+ MF 32-33
    VDpL (33)+
    VFsR (33)+, MF 1-33
    VHaI 1+
    VHcC 34+
    VKpL 19+
    VMaC 30+
    VMpL
    VNsC (2-12), (16-32)+
    VPcL
    VPwC 34+
    VRcP 32+
    VRoP 33+
    VRpL 1-2, (17-22)-(25-33)+
    VSpL (28-33)
    VStC
    VSuC 25+
    VTnC (32)-(34)
    VUnU 2-5, 8, 11-13
    VUnV 1-(2)-(7)-(9)-16, 18, 20
    VUtS 35+
    VWpL

NEGRO IN PRINT; BIBLIOGRAPHIC SURVEY.
   (Negro Bibliographic and Research Center, Inc.)
   Washington, D. C. v1, My 1965+
    AAM 1-6
    ATT 1+
    AU 1+
    GA 7+
    NcDurC 3
    NcElcU 2
    NcFayS 1
    NcGU 1
    NcRR 1+
    ScCLEA 5+
    ScOrC 4+
    TNF
    TNMe 1+
    TRR

(NEGRO IN PRINT; BIBLIOGRAPHIC SURVEY.)
      VCwM 1+
      VFsR 1+
      VHaI 2
      VUnU 1+


NEGRO IN THE UNITED STATES.
      ScRHW


NEGRO JOURNAL OF RELIGION.
   Wilberforce, Ohio.  v1, 1935+
      ATT   2
      GAU (1)
      TNF (1-4)


NEGRO LEADER.
      A-AR F 1911-N 1915


NEGRO LIFE.
   Houston, Texas.  1, Ja 1944+
      TNF (1-3)


NEGRO MAGAZINE.
      ATT


NEGRO MUSIC JOURNAL.
   Washington, D. C.  v1-2, (no1-15), S 1902-N 1903//
      GA 1-2 MF
      NcCU 1-2
      VHaI 1-2
      VNsC
      VUnV 1-(2)


NEGRO PROGRESS.
   (Published quarterly as a special feature of the
   out-reach ministry of Central Baptist Church)
   Wilmington, North Carolina.  v1, 1947
      NcRR 6-16
      VHaI (13), (15), (17)

NEGRO PROGRESS RECORD.
   (Negro Organization Society of Virginia) Hampton,
   Virginia.  vl, 1922
      VHaI (1-4), (6)

NEGRO QUARTERLY:  A REVIEW OF NEGRO LIFE AND CULTURE.
   New York.  1, Spring 1942-Winter/Spring 1943//
         AAM 1
         ATT 1
         GA 1 MF
         GACC 1
         NcCU 1
         NcDurC 1
         ScCLEA 1-
         ScU 1
         TNF 1
         VCoU 1
         VHaI (1)
         VMaC 1
         VStC
         VUnU 1
         VUnV 1

NEGRO SOUTH.
   New Orleans, Louisiana.  vl-10, N 10, 1937-D 1947//
      TNF (1945,47)

NEGRO STATESMAN.
   (National Council of Negro Republicans; Association
   for Negroes in American Industry) Philadelphia.
   N 1945-Jl 1948//?
      ATT 2
      GAU (1), (3)

NEGRO STORY; A MAGAZINE FOR ALL AMERICANS.
   Chicago.  vl-2, no3 My/Je 1944-Ap/My 1946//
      GA 1-2 MF
      NcCU 1-2
      ScU 1-2
      TNF 1-2

(NEGRO STORY; A MAGAZINE FOR ALL AMERICANS.)
    VHaI (1-2)
    VNsC (1-2)
    VUnV 1-(2)

NEGRO TRAVELER AND CONVENTIONEER.
    Chicago.  1, D 1944+
        GAU (2)
        VMaC 2, 4-113
        VRpL (17-19)+

NEGRO WOMAN'S WORLD.
    1934
        ATT 2

NEGRO WORKER.
    (Red International of Labor Unions.  International
    Trade Union Committee of Negro Workers) Hamburg,
    Germany.  1-2 Jl 15, 1928-29; (ns) v1-7, no7/8,
    Ja 1931-S/O 1937//
        ATT 1-7 MF
        GAMB 1-7 MF
        GAU 1-7
        TNF (4-7)
        VHaI (6-7)
        VUnU 1-7 MF

NEGRO WORLD.
    New York.  Jl 3, 1926-Je, 1933//
        ATT 1920-33 MF
        GAU 1926-33
        TMVH
        VHaI 1926-33 MF
        VUnU 1926-33 MF

NEGRO WORLD DIGEST.
    New York.  v1, no1-5, Jl-D 1940//
        GAU 1
        VHaI 1

111

NEGRO WORLD STATESMAN.
Philadelphia. vl, 1946+ See also Negro Statesman
TNF

NEGRO WRITER AND LITERARY REVIEW.
Toledo, Ohio. vl, nol, F/Mr 1948//
GAU

NEW AFRICA.
London. 1, Jl 1959+ (Formerly: Africa Trade and
Development)
GAU (2-8)

NEW AFRICAN LITERATURE AND THE ARTS.
New York. vl, 1969+
VUnV 1-2

NEW AGE.
Portland, Oregon.
VStC

NEW CHALLENGE.
Boston. vl-2, no2, Mr 1934-Fall 1937//? (vl-2, nol
as: Challenge; a literary quarterly)
ATT 1-2
GA 1-2 MF
NcCU 1-2
TNF (1-2)
VHaI 1-2
VNsC 1-2

NEW CRUSADER.
Chicago. w 1940+
ATT
TNF

NEW DAY.
Philadelphia. 1, 1936+
ATT (1-6) MF
GAU (3-6)

(NEW DAY.)
      TNF (2)
      VHaI 1-6 MF
      VUnU 1-6 MF

NEW ERA.
    Washington, D. C.  v1, 1912+
      TNF

NEW ERA MAGAZINE.
    Washington, D. C.  v1, 1936+
      TNF

NEW LADY:  REFLECTING A GREATER WAY OF LIVING.
    Hayward, California.  1966+
      NcCJ (6)
      TNF (1)

NEW NEGRO TRAVELER AND CONVENTIONEER:  MONTHLY MAGAZINE
OF THE NEGRO TRAVELER AND CONVENTIONEER AND HOTEL-MOTEL
RESTAURANT AND TAVERN WORLD.
    v1, 1953+
      NcElcU
      ScCOB (15)+
      ScOrC 16
      VHaI (15-16)

NEW ORLEANS DAILY CREOLE.
    d
      GAU Jl 1, 1856-Ja 10, 1857

NEW ORLEANS TRIBUNE.
    GAU My 2, 1865-F 28, 1869

NEW SOUTH.
    (Southern Regional Council) Atlanta, Georgia.  1,
    Ja 1946+
      ATT 1+
      GA 26
      GAU 1, (2-9), 10-17, (18-21)
      NcBuC 11+
      NcCQ

(NEW SOUTH.)
      NcDurC 5+
      NcFayS 13-18, 26+
      NcRM 13+
      NcRR 20-25
      NcRS 1+
      NcSalL 23+
      ScCOB (2, 4-6, 10-20)
      ScGAL 21+
      ScGRVF 16+
      ScNC 21+
      ScOrC (18-19, 21-23)+
      ScSpW 21+
      ScU 1-22, 23+ MF
      TJoS
      TNF (1-15), (16), (20), (22), 23
      TNMe 13-25+
      VCnC 21+
      VCoU (13-22), 26+
      VCwM 1+
      VFeC 25+
      VHaI (1)-(3-4)-(6-8)-(14-18)+
      VHoC 19-(20)-(23-26)+
      VMaC 21+
      VUnV
      VUtS 1+

NEW VISTAS.
    Chicago.  v1, no1-9, Je 1945-Ap 1946//
      TNF

NEW YORK AGE.
    w 1880+
      ATT Ja 5, 1905-F 27, 1960
      GAMB Ja 5, 1905-F 27, 1960
      GAU My 29, 1886-F 1960
      VHaI MF 1905-60
      VUnU MF 1905-60
      VStC

NEW YORK AMSTERDAM NEWS.
    w D 7, 1909+
        GAU 1962-64
        ScCOB
        ScOrC +
        TNF

NEWS FROM SOUTH AFRICA.
    New York.  1966+
        ScCOB
        ScRHW 1+

NEWS LETTER.
    (CWBM)
        TNDC

NEWSPIC.
    Birmingham, Alabama.  v1-7, no1, O 1940-Ja 1947//
        ATT 1-6
        TNF (1), (3), 4-(5-7)

NIGERIA:  A QUARTERLY MAGAZINE FOR EVERYONE INTERESTED
IN THE PROGRESS OF THE COUNTRY.
    Lagos, Nigeria.  no1, 1934+  (no1-8 as:  Nigerian
    Teacher)
        GAU 14, 37-39, 52-61, 67-71, 74-80
        VCwM no12-99
        VHaI no57, 72-73
        VUnV (74)

NIGERIA TRADE JOURNAL.
    Lagos, Nigeria.  1953+
        ATT (12)+
        GAU 4-5, (11-12)
        VHaI (11-12)

NIGERIAN GEOGRAPHICAL JOURNAL.
    Ibadan, Nigeria.  1957+
        VNsC

NIGERIAN JOURNAL OF ECONOMICS AND SOCIAL STUDIES.
    (Nigerian Economic Society) Ibadan, Nigeria.  vl,
    1959+
        VNsC

NILES WEEKLY REGISTER.
    Philadelphia.  7-52, S 1814-Ag 1837.  (Title varies:
    Niles National Register.  vl-76, no13, S 1811-
    S 1849//)
        TNF 1-76

NKOMBO.
    (Free Southern Theatre) New Orleans, Louisiana.
        NcElcU
        TNF

NON-SLAVEHOLDER.
    Philadelphia.  vl-5, 1846-50; ns vl-2, 1853-54//
        GA ns1-2 MF
        NcCU 1-5, ns1-2
        VNsC 1-5, ns1-2

NORFOLK JOURNAL AND GUIDE.
    Norfolk, Virginia.  1901+
        ATT S 30, 1916+
        ScCOB
        ScOrC

NORTH CAROLINA TEACHER'S ASSOCIATION NEWSLETTER.
        NcRR

NORTH CAROLINA TEACHER'S RECORD.
    Raleigh, North Carolina.  1, Ja 1930-Ja 1970//
        NcRR 34-41

NOTES NEGRO MAGAZINE.
        TNF
        VNsC

NURSERY BIBLE LESSONS.
    Nashville.
        TNSPB

NURSERY-KINDERGARTEN ACTIVITIES.
    Nashville.
        TNSPB

OBSERVER.
        ScSpW

OBSERVER.
    Baltimore.   1-2, N 29, 1806-D 26, 1807//
        ScU 1-2 MF

OBSERVER.
    New York.  no1-25, F 19-Ag 6, 1809//
        ScU 1-25 MF

OBSERVER.
    New York.  no1-28, O 14, 1810-Ap 21, 1811//?
        ScU 1-28

OKIKE.
    (Nwankwo-Ifejika & Co.) Enugu, Nigeria.  v1, Ap 1971+
        GA

OKLAHOMA EAGLE.
    Muskogee, Oklahoma.  w 1932+
        TNF

ON THE TRACK.
    (Association of American Railroads) Philadelphia.
    v1, 1952+
        NcRR
        VStC

OPINION-BLACK AND WHITE.
    1923
        ATT 1

OPPORTUNITY; A JOURNAL OF NEGRO LIFE.
    (National Urban League for Social Service Among
    Negroes) New York.  1, 1923-26, 1948//
        AAM 10-23
        ATT 1-27 MF

(OPPORTUNITY; A JOURNAL OF NEGRO LIFE.)
        AU 1-27
        GA 9-25, 1-27 MF
        GAMB 1-27 MF
        GAU 1-27
        NcCoB 5-23
        NcD 15+
        NcDurC 1-27 MF
        NcElcU
        NcFayS 1-27
        NcGU 1-27
        NcRR 14-26
        NcRS 1-27
        NcRSA 4-25
        NcU 1+
        ScCOB
        ScOrS 1-16, 17-27 MF
        ScU 1-27
        TNF 1-11, 13-26
        TNMe 1-27
        VCwM 1-27
        VHaI 1-26 MF 1-27
        VRpL 4-27
        VStC
        VUnU MF 1-27
        VUnV 1-20

OPPORTUNITY.
    (Office of Economic Opportunity) Washington, D. C.
    1971+
        GA 1

ORACLE.
    (Omega Psi Phi Fraternity) Oklahoma City, Oklahoma.
    v1, 1921+
        ATT 6+
        TNF (4-6), (8-12), (14-15), (17-19), (26-27),
         (31), (34-35), (37-38), (42)
        VHaI (38), (40), (43-44), (56-57)

OUR AFRICA.
        TNJ-S (2)

OUR BOOK-GOOD WILL MAGAZINE.
    Cleveland, Ohio.  vl-5, nol, Ap ?1941-Mr 1946//
        TNF

OUR NATIONAL FAMILY.
    (National Congress of Colored Parents and Teachers)
    Atlanta, Georgia.  1940+
        ATT 14-20
        NcRR (13)
        TNF (10-13), (15-20), (22-23)
        VHaI (12-13)-(15-16)-(21-22), (24-25)

OUR WORLD; A PICTURE MAGAZINE FOR THE WHOLE FAMILY.
    New York.  1, Ap 1946-10, 1955//
        ATT 1-10
        NcElcU 6-8
        NcRR 3-10
        TNF 1-(9-10)
        VHaI 1-(4)-(10)
        VStC
        VUnU 1-7
        VUtS (1-6)

OVERSEA EDUCATION.
    London.  1, 1929+
        TNF (15-19), (21-35)

PACE.
    Los Angeles.
        NcRR

PALMETTO LEADER.
        GAU F 5, 1949

PAN-AFRICA; JOURNAL OF AFRICAN LIFE AND THOUGHT.
    Manchester, England.  vl-12, no3-4, Ja 1947-48//
        ATT 1
        VHaI (1)

PAN-AFRICAN JOURNAL.
    New York.  1968+

(PAN-AFRICAN JOURNAL.)
      ScCOB 1+
      TNJ-S 1
      VCoU 4+
      VUnV 1-2

PANORAMA REVUE MENSULLA.
      TNF

PEOPLE'S ADVOCATE.
   Washington, D. C.
      VStC

PEOPLE'S VOICE.
   New York. 1942
      GAU O 24, 1942

PEP.
   (Negro Publisher, Editor and Printer) Chicago.  v1,
   1943
      TNF (1-3)
      VHaI (1-2)

PHILADELPHIA TRIBUNE.
   w N 2, 1884+
      GAU (66)
      ScCOB
      VStC

PHOENIX.
      TNF

PHYLON; THE ATLANTA UNIVERSITY REVIEW OF RACE AND
CULTURE.
   Atlanta, Georgia.  1, Ja 1940+
      AAM 1-5, 7-16, 18-20, 25-30
      ATT 1+
      AU 1
      GA 1-, 1-23 MF
      GACC 5, 15, 20-21, 24, 25, 27
      GASC 5-6
      GAU 1+, 17-29 MF

(PHYLON; THE ATLANTA UNIVERSITY....)
        NcBoA 29+
        NcCJ 23-24, 27+
        NcCoB 3, 11-20, 27-32
        NcCU 19-24, 26
        NcDur
        NcDurC 3+
        NcElcU
        NcFayS 1+ MF
        NcGU 1+
        NcGuG
        NcLA 1+
        NcRR 1+
        NcRS 1+
        NcRSA 25+
        NcRSH
        NcSalL 1+
        NcWS
        ScCLEA
        ScCOB
        ScGRVF 14, 23+
        ScOrC 1+
        ScOrS 17, 21-22, 26, 28, 1-30, 32-33, 34 MF
        ScRHW 23, 24, 26+
        ScU 1-33
        TJeCN 1+
        TJoS
        TM-SW 29+
        TNBK 21+
        TNF 1-7, 9-31+
        TNK
        TNL 8, 10, 14-15, 18-22, 24-25, 27
        TNLO
        TNM 19+
        TNMe 1+
        TRR
        VBrC (25)-(31)
        VCnC 31+
        VCoU 31+
        VCwM 1+
        VFsR 32+, MF 1-23, 26-31

(PHYLON; THE ATLANTA UNIVERSITY....)
        VHaI 1+
        VKpL (27)+
        VMaC 1+, MF 1-26
        VNsC 2-6, 8-9, 12, 14-21, 24+
        VRpL 1-(26)+
        VStC
        VUtS 3-12, 17, 24+
        VUnU 2-21; MF 22+
        VUnV 1+

PILOT.
    (Official Publication of the National Negro Insurance
    Association) Chicago.  v1, 1951+
        AAM 20
        NcCJ (21-22)
        TNF (1-2)
        VHaI (1-2), (15), (18)-(20)

PITTSBURGH COURIER.
    w 1910+
        AAM 1923
        ATT J 20, 1923+ MF
        GAU J 13, 1923-D 26, 1970
        NcCJ
        NcCoB
        NcD Ja 13, 1923+ MF
        NcDur
        NcDurC Ja 20, 1923+ MF
        NcFayS 1923+
        NcFB
        NcGU 1923+ MF
        NcRR 1967+
        NcRSH
        NcSalL 1911-1912, 1923-1972 MF
        S.D. Bishop
        ScCOB
        ScOrC 1910-1923 MF
        ScOrS 1923+, 2MF
        TKM
        TNF
        TN-H

(PITTSBURGH COURIER.)
   TNK 1923+ MF
   TNLO
   TNMa 1954-Jl 1969
   TNMe Ja 13, 1923-D 31, 1969 MF
   VHaI MF 1911-12, 1963+
   VMaC MF Ja 13, 1923+
   VNsC
   VRoP 1970+
   VStC
   VUnU MF 1911-12; 1923+

PLAIN TRUTH.
  Pasadena, California. 1934
   ATT 28

POST.
  Johannesburg, South Africa.
   NcRR

POSTAL ALLIANCE.
  (National Alliance of Postal Employees) St. Louis,
  Missouri. 1, 1915+
   ATT 20+
   TNF 28-30, 32-40
   VHaI (30-41)

PRESENCE AFRICAINE.
  Paris. no1, N/D 1947+
   ATT 25+
   GAU 1, 6-33, 37, 39
   TNF (1), 10-(14), 17, 19-24
   VCwM 57+
   VHaI 1-2, 9-21, 22+
   VNsC 15-18
   VUnV (10-23), 26+

PRIDE.
  Philadelphia. v1, 1966+
   GA 5+

PRIMARY ACTIVITIES.
    Chicago.  1-4, S 1936-Ap 1940//
        TNSPB

PRIMARY BIBLE LESSONS.
    Nashville.
        TNSPB

PRIMARY PUPIL'S EDITION OF VACATION CHURCH SCHOOL.
    Nashville.
        TNSPB

PRIMARY QUARTERLY.
    Nashville.
        TNBPB

PRINCE HALL MASONIC REVIEW.
        TNF

PROBLEMES D'AFRIQUE CENTRALE.
    Brussels.  vl-13 (nol-44) 1947-Ap 1959//
        ATT nos. 35-38

PROGRESS RECORD.
    (Negro Organization Society of Virginia, Inc.) 1930
        VHaI (12), (15), (17-20)
        VUnV 9-13, (14-15)

PULSE.
    Washington, D.C.  vl-6, no6, F 1943-Jl 1948//?
        ATT (1-6)
        TNF (3-5)

QUARTERLY ANTI-SLAVERY MAGAZINE.
    (American Anti-Slavery Society) New York.  1-2,
    O 1835-Jl 1837//
        ATT 1-2
        TNF 1-2

QUARTERLY BULLETIN OF AFRICAN MATERIALS.
    Boston University.  Boston.  vl, 1972//  (Formerly:
    Monthly Bulletin of African Materials)
        VHaI (1)

QUARTERLY JOURNAL.
Tallahassee, Florida. vl, 1932-
ATT 4-13
TNF (1-4), (6-8), 11, 12, (15-16)

QUARTERLY REVIEW OF HIGHER EDUCATION AMONG NEGROES.
(Johnson C. Smith University) Charlotte, North
Carolina. 1, Ja 1933-1969//?
AAM 34-36
ATT 1-36
GA 1-4 MF
GAU 1-(17)-(22)-(29)
NcCU 1-4
NcDurC 5+
NcElcU 15-34
NcFayS 7-36
NcRR (3), (28), (32-34)
NcRS 1+
NcSalL 4+
ScCOB
ScOrC (29-30, 32, 34, 36)
ScU 1-28
TMU 1-27
TNF 1-8, (11)-28
TNL 17, 21-25, 33
TNLO
VHaI 1-(12)-(17)-(21)-(30), (32)
VNsC 1-27
VStC
VUnU (1)-34, 37
VUnV 1-28

ROTC BULLETIN.
(Hampton Institute) Hampton, Virginia. vl, 1964+
VHaI (1-5)

RACE: DEVOTED TO SOCIAL, POLITICAL AND ECONOMIC EQUALITY.
(Conference on Social and Economic Aspects of the
Race Problem) New York. vl, no1-2, Winter 1935/36-
Summer 1936//
GA 1 MF
GAU (1)

(RACE: DEVOTED TO SOCIAL,....)
> NcCU 1
> TNF 1
> VHaI (1)
> VUnV 1-2

RACE.
> (Institute of Race Relations) London.  v1, 1959+
> AAM (10-11)
> ATT 6+
> NcElcU 12+
> TNMe 1+
> VCwM 5+
> VUnV +

RACE RELATIONS; A MONTHLY SUMMARY OF EVENTS AND TRENDS.
> (Fisk University.  Social Science Institute)
> Nashville.  v1-5, no9/12, Ap 1943-Je/D 1948//
> (Ag 1943-D 1946 as:  Monthly Summary of Events and
> Trends in Race Relations; Ja-Je 1947 as:  Events and
> Trends in Race Relations.  None published between
> Jl and O/N 1947)
> > GA
> > NcCU
> > NcDurC 1
> > NcGU 1-5
> > ScCOB 1, 7+
> > ScCoC 1-5
> > ScU 1-5
> > TNF 1+
> > TNJ-S (1-2), 3-5
> > VHaI 1-5
> > VNsC 1-5
> > VUnV (1)-5

RACE RELATIONS JOURNAL.
> (South African Institute of Race Relations)
> Johannesburg, South Africa.  1, N 1933+  (Formerly:
> Race Relations)
> > GAU (2), (14-18), (20), (25), (28)

RACE RELATIONS LAW REPORTER.
  (Vanderbilt University School of Law) Nashville.
  v1-12, no4, F 1956-Winter 1967//
     AAM 1-4
     ATT 1-2
     GA 2+
     GAU 1-(2), (3)-4-7-(8)-9-(10)-11
     NcCoB 1-5
     NcDurC 1-12
     NcElcU 1-11
     NcFayF 5+
     NcRR 1-12
     NcRS 1-12
     TMU 1-12
     TM-SW (15)+
     TNF 1-10
     TNJ-S 1-12
     VCoU 4-12
     VHaI 1-12
     VNsC 2-12
     VRaC 1-12
     VUnV 1-12
     VUtS 1-12

RACE RELATIONS LAW SURVEY.
  (Vanderbilt University. School of Law) Nashville.
  v1-3, no6, My 1969-Mr 1972//
     AAM 1
     ATT 1+
     GA 2+
     NcCoB 2
     NcRR 1
     NcSalL
     ScCOB
     TJeCN 1
     TJoS
     TMU 1+
     TNJ-S 1+
     TNF
     VBrC 1-3
     VHaI 1-3
     VMaC 1-3

(RACE RELATIONS LAW SURVEY.)
      VMcC 1-3
      VRaC 1-3
      VRmW 1-3
      VUnV 1-3
      VUtS 1-3

RACE RELATIONS NEWS.
    (South African Institute of Race Relations)
    Johannesburg, South Africa.  no1, Jl 1938+
      ATT 8-10
      TNF (1-6)-7-(8)-9-10-(11-13)-14-17-(18-19)-20-
      (21)

RACE RELATIONS REPORTER.
    (Race Relations Information Center) Nashville.  vl,
    1970+
      AAM 1
      ATT 1+
      GA
      NcElcU
      NcRR 2+
      NcWU 1+
      S.D. Bishop
      ScU
      VBrC (2)+
      VHaI (1)+
      VRmW 2+
      VUnV 1+

RACE TODAY.
    (Institute of Race Relations) London.  Vl, My 1969+
      GA 4+
      TNMe +
      VFsR 4+
      VUnV 3+

RACIAL DIGEST.
    Detroit, Michigan.  vl, 1942+
      TNF

RADICAL ABOLITIONIST.
New York.  v1-4, no5, Ag 1855-58//?  (Supersedes:
American Jubilee)
AAM 1-4
GA 1-4 MF
NcWU 2-4
ScU 1-4
VCoU 1-4
VHaI 1-4
VNsC 1-4
VUnV 1-4

RADICAL, in continuation of the Workingman's Advocate.
Granville, New Jersey.  v1-2, no4, 1841-Ap 1843//?
VUnV (1) MF

RECORDER.
Indianapolis, Indiana.  1897+
VStC

REPEVE; POLITIQUE, LITTERAIRE.
Port-au-Prince, Haiti.  v1-8, 1932-1939//
TNF

RELIGIOUS AND LITERARY REPOSITORY.
Annapolis, Maryland.  v1, no1-24, Ja 15-D 23, 1820//
ScU 1 MF

REPORT.
(UCMS Committee on Interim Developments in Negro
Church Life)
TNDC

REPORT FROM AFRICA.
(Sudan Interior Mission)
TNDC
TNJ-S

REPORT FROM NIGERIA.
(Church of Christ)
TNDC

REPORTER.
 New York. 1, Ap 26, 1949+
  ScCLP (26), 3 (6)-31
  ScCOB (31, 33-38)+
  ScCoC 20-38
  ScGRVF 7-38
  ScHaC (26, 27)-(32), 38
  ScNC 14-35-(36-37), 38
  ScSPC (13-17), 18-38
  ScSpW 1, 8-37

REPORTER EAST AFRICAN WEEKLY NEWS MAGAZINE.
 Nairobi, Kenya. v1, 1960+
  TNF (4-5)
  VHaI (2-4), (7)

REPOSITORY OF RELIGION AND LITERATURE AND SCIENCE AND
ART.
 Baltimore, Maryland. v1-5, no1, 1859-1863//?
  VUnV 4

REVIEW OF BLACK POLITICAL ECONOMY.
 (Black Economic Research Center) New York. 1970+
  GA 2+
  NcElcU 1+
  TRR
  VCoU (1)+
  VHaI 1+

REVOLUTION IN CIVIL RIGHTS.
  VNsC

REVUE DE LA SOCIETE HAITIENNE D'HISTOIRE DE GEOGRAPHIE
ET DU GEOLOGIE.
 Port-au-Prince, Haiti. v1, 1929
  VHaI (24-27), (29)

RHODESIA CALLING.
  TNJ-S (1)

RHYTHM MAGAZINE.
  NcElcU
  TNF

RICHMOND PLANET.
  w Richmond, Virginia. D? 1883+
    GAU Ja 5, 1895-S 29, 1900
    VStC (1890), 1891-1908, (1909)-Mr 28, 1931, Mr 17,
    1934-My 28, 1938

RIGHTS.
  (National Emergency Civil Liberties Committee)
  New York. v1, 1953+
    ScOrC (9-13-15)+
    VHaI (9-12)
    VUnV (3)

ROANOKE TRIBUNE.
  Roanoke, Virginia. 1938+
    VRoP 1970+

SCLC NEWSLETTER.
  (Southern Christian Leadership Conference) Atlanta,
  Georgia. v1, 1963+
    VHaI (1-2)

SACRAMENTO OBSERVER.
  Sacramento, California. 1962+
    NcFayS
    NcSalL
    ScCOB
    TNF
    VHaI +
    VUnU +

SAINT AUGUSTINE'S MESSENGER.
  (Society of the Divine Word) Bay St. Louis,
  Mississippi. v1, 1923+
    TNF (17), (20-33)
    VHaI (30-32)

SAINT LOUIS AMERICAN.
      w 1928+
            GAU 1960-64

SAINT LOUIS ARGUS.
      w 1912+
            NcDurC N 1951+

SAINT PAULITE.
      (Saint Paul College) Lawrenceville, Virginia.   vl,
      1957+
            VHaI (11-12)
            VUnV (3)-(4)

SAVANNAH TRIBUNE.
      Savannah, Georgia.   D 4, 1875+
            ATT D 4, 1875-O 7, 1943 MF
            GAU D 4, 1875-S 1960
            VHaI MF 1875-1943

SCHOLARSHIP.
      Washington, Kentucky.   vl, 1946
            TNF

SCHOOL TEACHER.
      Washington, D. C.   vl-2, 3, nol, 1909-S 1910//
            VUnV (2)

SCORE.
      Seattle, Washington.   1960+
            TNF

SEARCHLIGHT.
      Winston-Salem, North Carolina.   vl, 1910?+
            ATT 1-5

SECHABA.
      (African National Congress of South Africa) London.
      vl, 1967+
            GA 4+

SECRETARIAT.
   (National Urban League) New York.  1938
      ATT 9

SEEN AND HEARD.
   Philadelphia.  1-8 (no1-341) 1901-My 27, 1908//?
      VHaI MF 3 MF
      VUnU MF 1-4 MF

SENIOR BIBLE QUARTERLY.
   Nashville.
      TNSPB

SENTINEL.
   Raleigh, North Carolina.  Ag 8, 1865-F 27, 1877//
      ScU Ja 25, 1866-D 19, 1871 MF

SEPIA.
   (Sepia Publishing Company) Fort Worth, Texas.  v1,
   1952+  (Title varies:  Sepia USA)
      GA 3+
      NcDurC 12+
      NcFayC 21+
      NcSalL
      TNF (6-16)
      TRR
      VFsR 20+
      VFwW 20+
      VHaI 20+
      Voorhees
      VUnV 19+

SEPIA RECORD.
   Davenport, Iowa.  v1, 1944+
      TNF

SERVICE.
   (Tuskegee Normal and Industrial Institute) Tuskegee,
   Alabama.  v1-18, no12, Ag 1936-J1 1954//  (Supersedes:
   Tuskegee Messenger.  s2, v1-7 repeated in numbering)
      NcRR 17-(19)
      TNF (2), (4-11), (27)

(SERVICE.)
        VCwM 5-18
        VHaI 1-2, (5-8)
        VStC

SET.
        TNF

SHAW UNIVERSITY BULLETIN.
        Raleigh, North Carolina. vl, 1964+
        VHaI (2-3)

SIERRA LEONE STUDIES.
        (Sierra Leone Society) Freetown, Sierra Leone.
        1918+
        TNF (36-43)

SIERRA LEONEAN.
        (Government Information Service) Freetown, Sierra
        Leone.
        VHaI 1961-62

SILHOUETTE.
        Los Angeles. vl, 1938+
        ATT
        TNF

SLAVERY IN AMERICA: WITH NOTICES OF THE PRESENT STATE
OF SLAVERY AND SLAVE TRADE THROUGHOUT THE WORLD.
        London. nol-14, Jl 1836-Ag 1837//
        GA 1836-1837 MF
        NcCU 1836-1837
        VHaI 1836-1837
        VNsC 1836-1837

SOCIAL ACTION.
        (Council For Social Action of the Congregational and
        Christian Churches) Boston. 1, Mr 1935+
        TNDC 11-12

SOCIAL ACTION NEWSLETTER.
(United Christian Missionary Society) Indianapolis,
Indiana. 1, D 1937 +
TNDC

SOCIAL AND ECONOMIC STUDIES.
(Institute of Social and Economic Research. University of the West Indies) Mona, Jamaica, B. W. I.
v1, 1953+
VCwM 19+

SOCIAL WHIRL.
New York. 1, 1954+
TNF

SOCIETY FOR AFRICAN CHURCH HISTORY.
Bulletin. Nsukka, Nigeria. 1, Ap 1963+
TNJ-S 1-(2)
VNsC

SOMETHING.
TNF

SOULBOOK.
(Soulbook, Inc.) Berkeley, California. 1965+
NcElcU
VCoU 7+
VFsR 8

SOUL FORCE.
(Southern Christian Leadership Conference) Atlanta,
Georgia. 1968?+
ATT 2+
GA 4+
TMU 4+
TM-SW 2+

SOUL ILLUSTRATED.
Los Angeles. 1968+ (Including Soul Newspaper)
NcElcU

SOUTH AFRICAN CHRISTIAN.
(Church of Christ Literature Services) East London,
South Africa. 1927+
TNDC 2-3, 37+

SOUTH AFRICAN DIGEST.
Pretoria, South Africa. v1, 1956+
NcDurC 9+
TNDC (10-13)

SOUTH AFRICAN INSTITUTE OF RACE RELATIONS.
Johannesburg, South Africa. Annual Report. 1,
1930+
TNF 14-15, 17, 19-21

SOUTH AFRICAN JOURNAL OF ECONOMICS.
Johannesburg, South Africa. 1, Mr, 1933+
VCwM 34+

SOUTH AFRICAN JOURNAL OF SCIENCE.
(South African Association for the Advancement of
Science) Cape Town, South Africa. 1, 1903+ (1-5,
1903-08 as: The Society's Report)
VCwM 62+
VUnV 42-43, 45, (47-48), (51-53)-(59)

SOUTH AFRICAN OUTLOOK.
(United Free Church of Scotland Mission) Lovedale,
South Africa. (51, 1921 as: Christian Express. A
journal of missionary news and Christian work)
ATT 75
TNF (64), (75)
TNJ-S (59), 60, (61), 62-63, (64-67), 68-69, (70),
71, (72-73), 74-75, (76), 77-96, (97-98) 99+
VHaI 68-(69)

SOUTH AFRICAN PANORAMA.
Pretoria, South Africa. v1, 1956+
TNF (5-14)
VCwM 15+
VFsR (16)+

SOUTH AFRICAN POST.
    VNsC

SOUTH AFRICAN SCOPE.
    (South African Information Service) New York.  v1,
    1958+
        NcDurC 1+
        ScCOB 11+
        ScOrS
        ScSPW 1+
        TNF (1-11)
        TNJ-S (1), 2-4, (5), 6-9, 11+
        VHaI (1-2), (4-6)-(9)-(13-14)+
        VMbC 14+

SOUTH AFRICAN SENTINEL.
    TNDC

SOUTH AFRICAN TORCH.
    (South African Church of Christ Mission)
        TNDC

SOUTH TODAY.
    (Leadership Project of the Southern Regional Council)
    Atlanta, Georgia.  v1, 1969+
        GA 2+
        NcGU 1+
        NcRR 1+
        NcWU
        TM-SW 1+
        TN
        TNF

SOUTHERN AGE.
    Atlanta, Georgia.
        GAU 1897

SOUTHERN BIVOUAC:  A MONTHLY LITERARY AND HISTORICAL
MAGAZINE.
    Louisville.  1-5, S 1882-My 1887//
        TNF (2-5)

SOUTHERN COURIER.
   w vl, 1965
      ATT 1-4
      AU 1-(2)-4

SOUTHERN EDUCATION.
   (Southern Education Board) Knoxville, Tennessee.  vl,
   nol-20, Mr-D 1903//
      VHaI nol-7, 10-19

SOUTHERN EDUCATION REPORT.
   (Southern Education Reporting Service) Nashville.
   vl, nol, 1965-v4, 1969//  (Formerly:  Southern School
   News.  S 1954-Je 1965)
      ATT 1+
      GAU 1-4
      NcDurC 1+
      NcRR 1-5
      NcWU 1-4
      ScCOB (2-3)+
      ScCoC 1+
      ScGRVF 1+
      ScNC 1+
      ScOrS 2-3
      TJoS
      TNF 1-5
      TNJ-S 1-2-(3)-4
      VFeC 1-4
      VHaI 1-4
      VHsC 1-4
      VMaC 1-4
      VRmW 1-4
      VRpL 1-4
      VStC
      VUnV 1-4
      VUtS 1-(2-4)

SOUTHERN FRONTIER.
   (Commission on Interracial Cooperation) Atlanta,
   Georgia.  1, Ja 1940+
      AAM
      APL

(SOUTHERN FRONTIER.)
        ATT
        NcCU 1-6
        ScU
        TNF (2-3, 5)
        VCoU 1-6
        VHaI 1-6
        VMaC 1-6
        VNsC 1-6
        VUnV (1-2)-6
        VUtS (1-6)

SOUTHERN INDEPENDENCE.
    Selma, Alabama
        A-AR Ap 23-My 8, 1886

SOUTHERN LETTER:  DEVOTED TO THE EDUCATION OF THE HAND,
HEAD AND HEART.
    (Tuskegee Normal and Industrial Institute) Tuskegee,
    Alabama.  v1-47, no8/9, 1884-Ag/S 1931//  (v34,
    no12, v47, no7 never published)
        VHaI 22-23, 25, (30-37)

SOUTHERN LITERARY MESSENGER:  DEVOTED TO EVERY DEPARTMENT
OF LITERATURE AND FINE ARTS.
    Richmond, Virginia.  1-38, Ag 1834-Je 1864//
        TNF 1-38

SOUTHERN NEWS.
    Atlanta, Georgia.  v1, 1923?+
        TNF

SOUTHERN NEWSLETTER.
    v1, 1956+
        ATT 2-4
        TNF (3)

SOUTHERN OBSERVER.
    v1, 1959
        ATT 1-2
        NcRR (6-8)
        TNF (4-7)

SOUTHERN PATRIOT.
   (Southern Conference for Human Welfare) Nashville.
   1, D 1942+
      ATT 1+
      AU 2-3, 10-12, (13-15), 16
      NcDurC 16+
      NcRR 22+
      TNF (5), (8-16), 18, 20-23, (24-26)
      VHaI (4), 14-(15)-(17), (19)-(21-22)+

SOUTHERN PRESBYTERIAN REVIEW.
   Columbia, South Carolina.  1-36, 1847-85//
      TNF 1-2, 17-21

SOUTHERN QUARTERLY REVIEW.
   New Orleans, Louisiana.  1-30, Ja 1842-F 1857//
   (O 1856 never published)
      TNF 1, 13, (20) - (26-27)

SOUTHERN REVIEW.
   Baton Rouge, Louisiana.  1935-1942; 1965+
      TNF

SOUTHERN SCHOOL NEWS.
   (Southern Education Reporting Service)  Nashville.
   v1-11, no12, S 1954-Je 1965//  (Superseded by:
   Southern Education Report)
      ATT 1-10
      NcDurC 1-7
      NcFayS 1-7
      NcGrE 3-(9)-10-(11)
      NcRM 1-11
      NcRR 1-11
      ScCOC 1-7, (8, 9), 10, 11
      ScNC (1), 2-11
      ScSPC 1-8
      ScSpW 2-11
      TNF 1-11
      TNMe 1
      TNJ-S 1-11
      VHaI 1-11

(SOUTHERN SCHOOL NEWS.)
        VHsC 1-11
        VMaC 1, (2), 3-11
        VRmW 1-11
        VRpL (1)-11
        VUnV 1-11
        VUtS 1-11

SOUTHERN SCHOOL REPORT.
    v1, 1965
        NcDurC 1+

SOUTHERN SENTINEL.
    Atlanta, Georgia.  v1, 1863
        GAU 1891, Ja 1891
        ScU Ap 11, 1863

SOUTHERN WORKMAN.
    (Hampton Normal and Agricultural Institute) Hampton,
    Virginia.  v1-68, no7, 1872-Jl 1939//
        ATT 1-68 MF
        GAU 1-68
        NcDurC 27-68
        NcGrE 60-62
        NcGU 53-68
        ScOrS 1-68
        TNF 28-70
        VCwM 47-68; MF 1-46
        VHaI 1-68; MF 1-68
        VMuC (29)-(37)
        VStC
        VUnV MF 1-68
        VUtS (30-31, 35, 60-65)
        VUnU MF 1-68

SOUTHWESTERN JOURNAL.
    Lawton, Oklahoma.  1, My 1944+
        TNF (2-5)+

SPADE.
        TNF+

SPELMAN COLLEGE BULLETIN.
Atlanta, Georgia.  1936-1971
GASC

SPELMAN MESSENGER.
(Spelman College) Atlanta, Georgia.  1, 1885+
GASC 43, 86
GAU 1-48, 50, 52, 55-80
TNF 49-51, 53-56, 66-71, 75
VHaI (72), (75), 78-(81)-(84-87)

SPHINX.
(Alpha Phi Alpha Fraternity, Inc.) Chicago.  v1,
1915+
AAM (55-56)
ATT 24+
NcCJ (56-57)
TNF 2-3, 9, 15-20, 23, 32-41
VHaI (39-40), (42), (50-51)

SPIRIT:  A MAGAZINE OF VERSE.
New York.  1, Mr 1934+
TNMe 30+

SPOKEN WORD.
Los Angeles.  v1-3, no81, O 20, 1934-Jl 31, 1937//
TNF 1-3

SPOTLIGHT.
TNF

SPOTLIGHT ON AFRICA.
(Council on African Affairs) New York.  v1-14, no5,
Jl 15, 1942-My 1955//
TNF (14)
VHaI (3-7)

STANDARD AND DIGGERS NEWS.
Johannesburg, South Africa.  O 2, 1899-My 31, 1900
ATT MF 1899-1900
VHaI MF 1899-1900
VUnU MF 1899-1900

STAR OF ZION.
   (African Methodist Episcopal Zion Church in America)
   Charlotte, North Carolina.  1, 1876+
      GAU 32, 52, 64, 68, 72, 86
      NcSalL MF 21-93
      TNF

STAR REVIEW.
   California.  1914+  (Formerly:  Watts Star Review)
      TNF
      VHaI +

STATE FEDERATION OF COLORED WOMEN'S CLUBS.
   Proceedings.  1935-1943
      ATT

STUDENT VOICE.
   (Jarvis Christian College) Hawkins, Texas.
      TNDC

STUDENT VOICE.
   (Student Non-Violent Co-Ordinating Committee)
   Atlanta, Georgia.  1, Je 1960+
      ATT 5

STUDIES IN BLACK LITERATURE.
   (University of Virginia) Fredericksburg, Virginia.
   v1, 1970+
      GA 2+
      NcElcU
      VCoU 1+
      VCwM 1+
      VHsC 1+
      VMwC 1+
      VUnU 1+

STUDIES IN RACE AND NATION.
   (Center On International Race Relations.  University
   of Denver) Denver, Colorado.  v1, 1969+
      VCoU 3+

SUNDAY SCHOOL INFORMER.
Nashville.
TNF
TNSPB +

SUPREME LIBERTY GUARDIAN.
Chicago.
GAU Ap 1949

T. C. B.
(Third World Magazine of S.U.N.Y. at Binghamton)
Binghamton, New York.
NcElcU

TAN.
Chicago.  1950-1971//
NcCJ (20), (22)
ScCOB
TMH
TNG (12-16)
VHaI (21)-22
VUsN +

TEACHER.
Nashville.
TNBPB

TEACHER'S MANUAL SERIES OF VACATION CHURCH SCHOOL.
Nashville.
TNSPB

TEXAS STANDARD.
Fort Worth, Texas.  vl, 1926?+
TNF

TONES AND OVERTONES.
(Alabama State College for Negroes) Montgomery,
Alabama.  1, Fall 1953+
TNF

TOUGALOO NEWS.
   (Tougaloo College) Tougaloo, Mississippi.  1871+
      TNDC

TOUGAZETTE.
   (Southern Christian College) Tougaloo, Mississippi.
      TNDC

TOURIST:  A LITERARY AND ANTI-SLAVERY JOURNAL.
   London.  vl, nol-44, S 17, 1832-My 27, 1883//
      TNF 1

TOWARD FREEDOM:  A NEWSLETTER ON NEW NATIONS.
   Chicago.  vl, 1952+
      VHaI (6)-(8-10)-(15)-(18)+

TRANSITION.
      TNF

TRAVEL.
   New York.  1, Jl 1901+
      TNF 63

TRIBUNE.
      ATT

TRIBUNE DE LA NEW ORLEANS.
      TNF

TRI-STATE DEFENDER.
   Memphis, Tennessee.  w 1951+
      TM-SW
      TNLO
      TNMe

TRUTH.
      A-AR N 5, 1903-Jl 3, 1909

TRUTH MESSENGER.
   Los Angeles.  vl, 1899?+
      TNF

TUESDAY.
   (Monthly supplement to twenty metropolitan newspapers) Chicago.  1965+
      AAM 6-7
      ATT 6+
      TNF (3)
      TN-E
      TNLO
      VHaI (3)+
      VPwC +
      VUnU (1-5)+
      VUnV (1-5)+

TUSCALOOSA CHRONICLE.
   Tuscaloosa, Alabama.  Ja 7, 1896-99//
      AU O 1896-J 1899

TUSKEGEE HERALD.
   Tuskegee, Alabama.
      ATT

TUSKEGEE INSTITUTE RECORDS AND RESEARCH PAMPHLETS.
   Tuskegee, Alabama.
      VUnV 1-10

TUSKEGEE MESSENGER.
   (Tuskegee Normal and Industrial Institute) Tuskegee,
   Alabama.  v1-12, no10/12 Ag 1924 O/D 1936//
   (Formed by the union of Tuskegee Student and Rural
   Messenger.  Superseded by:  Service)
      TNF (1-8)-11-(12)
      VHaI 1-(6)-12

TUSKEGEE NEWS.
   ATT

TUSKEGEE STUDENT.
   (Tuskegee Normal and Industrial Institute) Tuskegee,
   Alabama.  v1-34, no6, 1884-Je 1924//  (United with:
   Rural Messenger to form:  Tuskegee Messenger)

(TUSKEGEE STUDENT.)
    A-AR (24), (28)
    TNF (33-34)
    VHaI (12), 15-(18-22)-25, 28-(29-34)

TUSKEGEE VETERINARIAN.
    (Tuskegee Institute Chapter of the American Veter-
    inary Medical Association) Tuskegee Institute,
    Alabama.  v1, 1952+
    VHaI 5-(7-8)-9

ULICO.
    (Official organ of Universal Life Insurance Co.)
    Memphis, Tennessee.  1, 1951+
    TNF
    VUnU 20+

UGANDA JOURNAL.
    (Uganda Society) Kampala, Uganda.  1, Ja 1934+
    TNF

UMBOWO.
    TNJ-S (18-20, 22-23)

UMBRA.
    New York.  v1, 1963+
    TNF

UNIONTOWN NEWS.
    A-AR

U.S. NEGRO WORLD.
    New York.  1, 1960+  (Formerly:  American Negro
    Reference Guide)
    AAM 10-11
    NcDurC 3+
    NcElcU
    VHaI (3-4)
    VUnV 3-4

UNIVERSITY HERALD.
Ibadan, Nigeria. 1, 1948
ATT 2

URBAN AND SOCIAL CHANGE REVIEW.
(Boston College) Chestnut Hill, Massachusetts. 1,
1967+ (Formerly: Institute of Human Sciences.
Review)
GA 4+

URBAN LEAGUE BULLETIN.
New York. v1-12, no4, 1911-0 1922// (1-10 as the:
League's Bulletin. Superseded by: Opportunity)
ATT 11

URBAN WEST.
San Francisco. 1, 1967+
NcFayS
TNJ-S (1), 2+

URBANITE.
New York. v1, 1961
TNF (1)
VUnU 1+

VANGUARD.
TNF

VARIA.
Durham, North Carolina. v1, 1966+
NcDurC
NcRR

VETEGEE.
(Veterans Administration Hospital) Tuskegee,
Alabama. 1958+
ATT

VIE AFRICANIE.
Paris. v1, Mr/Ap 1959+
TNF

VINTAGE JAZZ MART.
  London.
  TNF

VIRGINIA EDUCATION BULLETIN.
  (Virginia Teacher's Association) Richmond, Virginia.
  1, 1919?  (Formerly:  Virginia Teacher's Bulletin)
    TNF
    VHaI
    VUnV (7), (11), (14), (15)-(18), (20), (36-38)

VIRGINIA TEACHER'S BULLETIN.
  (Virginia State Teacher's Association) Newport News,
  Virginia.  v1, 1924
    ATT 20-21
    VHaI (5)-(19-21)-22

VISION.
  1, 1936
    ScGRVF

VISION.
  (Atlanta Life Insurance Company) Atlanta, Georgia.
  v1, 1968+
    VHaI 1-(2-3)
    VUnU 2+

VISION OF MISSIONS.
  (African Methodist Episcopal Church Missionary
  Department) New York.  1, 1892+
    GAU (1), (4), (5), (7)

VOICE.
  Jamaica, New York.  1959
    ScSpW 8+

VOICE OF ETHIOPIA.
  (Ethiopian World Federation, Inc.) New York.  1,
  1937+
    GAU (3), (4)

VOICE OF THE NEGRO:  AN ILLUSTRATED MONTHLY MAGAZINE.
Atlanta, Georgia.  vl-4, no2, 1904-Mr 1907// (v3,
noll-v4, no2, N 1906-Mr 1907 as:  Voice.  Chicago)
  AAM 1-4
  ATT 1-4 MF
  GAU 1-4 MF
  TNF 1-3
  VHaI 1-3 MF
  VUnU 1-3 MF
  VUnV 1-(2)-4

VOICE OF THE PEOPLE.
  (Name changed to Weekly Voice N 4, 1916.  Changed
  back to Voice of the People Ja 1918)
  A-AR J 17, 1916-D 20, 1919; Ja 7-14, 1922, Ag 5,
    19, 1922

WASHINGTON BEE.
  w Washington, D. C.  Je 3, 1882-Ja 21, 1922//
  GAU Je 10, 1882-Ja 21, 1922
  VStC

WASU.
  (West African Students Union of Great Britain and
  Ireland) London.  vl, 1926+
  TNF

WATOTO MAGAZINE.
  Philadelphia, Pennsylvania.
  NcElcU

WEEKLY ADVOCATE.
  New York.  vl-3, no23, Ja 7, 1837-39//
  VHaI 1-3

WEEKLY PELICAN.
  w New Orleans, Louisiana.  1886-89//
  VStC

WEEKLY REVIEW.
  GAU 1960-63

WEEKLY VOICE.
　　A-AR N 4, 1916-Ag 25, 1917; Ja 10, 1920-D 17, 1921

WELFARE REPORTER.
　　Trenton, New Jersey. 1, 1946
　　　TNF (3-5), (5-6), 7-9, (10-14), 15-18

WEST AFRICA: A WEEKLY NEWSPAPER.
　　London. vl, F 3, 1917+ (Supersedes African Mail)
　　　NcRSH
　　　ScCOB 52
　　　ScU (1-12) MF
　　　VCwM 40-42, 44+
　　　VNsC 4-5

WEST AFRICA LINK.
　　Lagos, Nigeria. vl, 1964+
　　　TNJ-S (1-2)

WEST AFRICAN JOURNAL OF EDUCATION.
　　(University of Ibadan) Ibadan, Nigeria. vl, 1957+
　　　NcRR (6), (11)
　　　VNsC 14+

WEST AFRICAN PILOT.
　　Lagos, Yaba, Nigeria.
　　　ATT
　　　GAU
　　　VHaI +

WEST AFRICAN REVIEW.
　　Liverpool, England. vl-11, no51, 1922-D 1930; s2,
　　v3, no53, Ja 1931+ (-My 1931 as Elders Review of
　　West Affairs; Je-Ag 1931: Elders West African
　　Review)
　　　TNF (15-19), 21, 22, 26-27, (29), 31, (33-34)
　　　VHaI (31-32)

WEST INDIES CHRONICLE.
　　(West India Committee) London. 1, 1886+ (Super-
　　sedes: West India Committee Chronicle)
　　　VCwM 84+

WESTERN CHRISTIAN RECORDER.
    Kansas City, Kansas.
      GAU (1910)

WESTERN INFORMANT.
    Los Angeles, California.  v1, 0 1936+
      TNF

WHETSTONE.
    (North Carolina Mutual Life Insurance Company)
    Durham, North Carolina.  1, 1923+
      ATT
      GAU (19-20), (25), (27-33), 34-(43)
      NcCJ 49+
      NcDur
      NcDurC
      NcFayS
      NcRR 38+
      ScCOB
      TNF (16), (19-20), (26), (28)-36-(37)-41
      VHaI (28-29)-(33)-(36-37)-(43)+
      VStC
      VUnU (33), (46-48)+

WIDE AWAKE.
    A-AR Je 17, 1898; F 14, 1900-Je 12, 1900

WILBERFORCE UNIVERSITY QUARTERLY.
    Wilberforce, Ohio.  v1-3, no4, D 1939-D 1942//
      NcRR 2-3
      TNF (1-3)
      VHaI (1)-(3)
      VStC

WILMINGTON JOURNAL.
    1, 1944
      NcDurC 20+
      NcElcU
      NcFayS 23+
      NcRR 24+
      NcUW 26

WOMAN'S NATIONAL MAGAZINE.
    Chicago.  vl-8, no6, 1933-N 1941//?
        TNF (5-6)
        VHaI (4-9)

WOMAN'S VOICE.
    Philadelphia.  vl, 1920
        TNF (3-4), (20-21)
        VHaI (2-3)

WOODMEN BANNER.
    Mt. Morris, Illinois.  vl, 1914?+
        TNF

WORKER'S VOICE.
    St. John, Antigua.
        ATT Ja 3, 1965-D 31, 1967 MF

WORLD'S MESSENGER.
    Ft. Worth, Texas.  1, 1944
        ATT 5

YOUNG ADULT QUARTERLY.
    Nashville.
        TNBPB

YOUNG PEOPLE'S QUARTERLY.
    Nashville.
        TNBPB

ZAIRE.
    Brussels.  vl, 1947+
        TNJ-S 1-4, (15)

ZAMBIA.
    (Zambia Information Services) Lusaka, Zambia.
    N 1964-Mr 1969//
        VHaI 2-4